D1127314

The Learning Society

The
Learning Society

Torsten Husén

with a Foreword by
W. Kenneth Richmond

Methuen & Co Ltd

WITHDRAWN

SHENANDOAH COLLEGE
LIBRARY
WINCHESTER, VA.

First published 1974
by Methuen & Co Ltd
11 New Fetter Lane, London EC4
© 1974 Torsten Husén
Printed in Great Britain
by Richard Clay (The Chaucer Press) Ltd
Bungay, Suffolk

SBN (hardbound) 416 79490 4
SBN (paperback) 416 79500 5

This title is available in both hardbound and
paperback editions. The paperback edition is sold
subject to the condition that it shall not, by
way of trade or otherwise, be lent, re-sold, hired out
or otherwise circulated in any form of binding or cover
other than that in which it is published and without a
similar condition including this condition being
imposed on the subsequent purchaser

Distributed in the USA by
Harper & Row Publishers, Inc.
Barnes & Noble Import Division

LA   Husén, Torsten
132
.H82   The learning
              society.

370 H956L

Contents

Foreword

The author of these essays may well be reckoned one of the most distinguished educationists in Europe today, a man for all nations, one who rightly commands a worldwide reputation, who combines the research-based expertise of a psychologist like Jerome Bruner with the social vision of a politician like Edgar Faure. Husén's curriculum vitae is, to say the least of it, illustrious; and merely to list the various posts he has held is enough to indicate that here is no ordinary academic.

Graduating as a BA at the University of Lund in 1937, PhD in 1944, Torsten Husén first served as an Assistant in the department of psychology in that university, (1938–44), later as a psychologist with the Swedish Armed Forces (1944–8). Appointed as an Associate Professor in 1947, then as Research Professor of Education at the University of Stockholm (1953–71), he was actively engaged in research and development – in school reorganization, in curriculum reform, in methodology, in the applications of educational technology – during the hectic period in which Sweden ranked as *the* pacemaker in the field of educational innovation. This work provides the substance of his book, *Educational*

Research and Educational Change. As Director of the Institute for Educational Research (1956–71), however, Husén's wide interests and immense energies have never been confined to his homeland: as he says, 'the defeat of present-day provincialism is necessary if the world is to survive.' He has travelled extensively and campaigned tirelessly in the cause of the internationalization of education. Not surprisingly, the dynamism of the New World has always attracted him and on more than one occasion he has taken time off from his official duties in order to teach and conduct research as a visiting professor in North American institutions of higher learning. Thanks to this, English is now his second language. In recognition of the high esteem in which he is held in the USA the National Academy of Education made him a Foreign Associate, the University of Chicago awarded him an honorary LLD, and Teachers College, Columbia, decorated him with its Medal for Distinguished Service in Education.

Since 1962, Husén has been Chairman of the International Association for the Evaluation of Educational Achievement (IEA) and, since 1970, Chairman of the governing body of the International Institute for Educational Planning in Paris. The former body's first report on *The International Study of Achievement in Mathematics,* published in 1967, aroused very considerable interest, as have subsequent IEA reports on general science, reading and other school subjects. Husén is the author of some forty books, mostly research monographs. He has written on adolescence, ability and environment, differentiation problems in comprehensive schools, curriculum development in mathematics, physics, chemistry and civics, twin research and other topics.

Latterly, the focus of his attention has shifted from the limited sector occupied by the learner's school career and is now trained more and more on the prospects opening up in the field of lifelong education. For this and other

reasons Husén was appointed to a personal chair of
international education at Stockholm in 1971 and became
Director of the Institute for the Study of International
Problems in Education. It is entirely fitting, therefore,
that his valedictory address on that occasion should
provide the first essay in *The Learning Society*. Complacent
readers should be warned in advance that unless they
come to terms with the viewpoint so trenchantly expressed
in the opening paragraph – a sober indictment of the vice
which permits us to treat education and schooling as if
they were somehow interchangeable terms – they are
unlikely to grasp the significant trends in Husén's thought.

Husén may not be 'the Einstein of education' as one of
his Swedish newspaper critics has ironically dubbed him,
but he certainly resembles Einstein in refusing to accept
axioms which the vast majority of his colleagues would
never dream of questioning. Unlike the deschoolers,
whose radicalism takes the form of sweeping assertions
without any regard for the need for empirical proof,
Husén's rejection of conventional wisdom is founded on
hard-won, systematic evidence. It is tempting to say that
what he does not know about the methods and findings
of educational research is not worth knowing: after all,
for years he has occupied a unique position as the person
chiefly responsible for co-ordinating and reporting the
mass of data obtained from IEA projects in many different
countries. Some of the conclusions he draws from all this
evidence, nevertheless, are likely to prove unwelcome to
the rank and file of educationists, not least those engaged
in the work of teacher training.

Does amount of instruction make a difference, he asks?
Most teachers, needless to say, are convinced that it does.
Four hours of algebra or German per week are better than
two – absolutely essential if standards are to be maintained,
they insist – which explains why they feel so aggrieved
when asked to give up a period of their precious time in

order to make room for other claimants in an overcrowded curriculum. By the same token, full-time school attendance is held to be necessarily superior to half-time, ('CHILDREN MISS EDUCATION' scream the headlines whenever a hard-pressed LEA finds it necessary to operate double shifts because of a temporary shortage of teachers) ; and nowadays even the pupil's social status, not to mention his life earnings, tends to be measured in terms of the length of his school life. On the face of it, 'Does amount of instruction make a difference ?' seems a silly question. Husén's answer amounts to saying that the difference is nothing like so great as is commonly supposed. The inference is that the importance attached to schooling is exaggerated, and that the habit of supposing that most learning takes place as a result of classroom instruction owes more to pedagogue's pride than to any sounder rationale.

Again, one of the articles of faith to which educationists have unhesitatingly subscribed hitherto affirms that the quality of any education system ultimately depends upon the level of professional competence of its teachers. If 'competence' is taken as meaning the efficient discharge of the teacher's traditionally didactic role this is another axiom which Husén would cheerfully reject. From now on (in this and in everything else his frames of reference are characteristically forward-looking) the onus for learning will lie with the individual pupil rather than with the teacher, whose main function, increasingly, will be that of an *animateur* – a provider of learning opportunities. So far as the curriculum is concerned the emphasis will be on the acquisition of adaptive skills – learning how to learn – rather than on 'content' subjects. Gone for ever is the notion that the basic training which the pupil receives in school will provide him with an adequate preparation which will serve him for the rest of his life. Gone, too, the concept of education as a process restricted to the

years of infancy, childhood and youth, a concept typified
by Durkheim's definition of it as 'the influence exercised
by adult generations on those that are not yet ready for
social life'. In its place we are asked to envisage a theory
and practice of a life of learning which begins at the
moment of birth and continues, as Illich says, 'up to, and
in the moment, of my death'.

Significantly, English usage is still left fumbling for an
appropriate term to designate this emergent concept. It is
true that the idea of education as a continuous process
was written into the 1944 Education Act, but the
revolutionary nature of its implications and ways and
means of implementing it have not given rise to the kind
of vigorous public debate which has been going on in
France, for example, during recent decades. To British
ways of thinking, 'permanent education' has faintly
authoritarian overtones, apt to conjure up horrific visions
of compulsory schooling for babes in arms and compulsory
courses for geriatrics. 'Continuing education' is too
awkward. 'Recurrent education' means something quite
different — re-treads for oldies — altogether less
comprehensive than the global concept that is needed.
'Lifelong learning' sounds better, the only trouble being
that it is so vague as to be in danger of identifying itself
with a simplistic philosophy of we-live-and-learn. So, as
usual, the Englishman compromises and settles for calling
it lifelong education. In any case, what's in a name, he
asks? It is arguable that the British genius is essentially
empirical and that while educationists in other countries
have been addressing themselves to the theoretical aspects
and problems of planification we have been busy getting
down to practicalities — witness the proliferation of adult
and further education, industrial training, nursery play
groups, community services, not to mention the Open
University (which posterity may see as the late twentieth
century's most significant breakthrough in the search for

a new institutional framework suited to an age of technology).

For all that, the urgent need is for an overarching theory to encompass all the varied agencies and activities, pre-school as well as post-school, voluntary as well as statutory, informal as well as formal, which together make up the expanding universe of lifelong education. To date, relatively few British educationists have felt it necessary to raise their sights as men like Edgar Faure, Paul Legrand, Bertrand Schwartz and Jean Le Veugle have done in France, Aldo Visalberghi, Giovanni Gozzer and Mauro Laeng in Italy, Bogdan Suchodolski in Poland, or Torsten Husén in Sweden. The hard truth is that professional educationists in this country are ill-prepared to face up to the unprecedented situation with which they are suddenly confronted. This is partly because of insular-mindedness, partly because, as McLuhan puts it, 'we are all technological idiots in terms of the new situation', but mainly because the study of education has grown up in institutions devoted more or less exclusively to the training of teachers. As a result, we find it difficult to rid ourselves of the notion that, when all is said and done, education is really only for the *young*: as a result, too, we are left with an educational psychology which largely interprets itself as *child* development – kid's stuff. Concerning the human life cycle as a whole, particularly now that we are entering an era in which leisure, not work, will be the central element, we are woefully ignorant. Ignorant, too, and strangely incurious, about the effects of the information revolution which are already transforming values, attitudes and lifestyles.

The Learning Society may help to correct this myopic outlook. As a contribution to the growing literature on lifelong education, it deserves to be placed alongside the 1972 UNESCO report *Apprendre à Être* (Learning to Be) a document which has aroused widespread debate on the

Continent and precious little so far, apparently, in Britain.
In many respects, Husén's futurology is a good deal less
utopian than the Faure Commission's – less idealistic, even,
than Etzioni's in *The Active Society*. Thus, despite his
disenchantment with the efficacy of formal instruction, he
believes that the school will continue to play a dominant
role; and despite his zeal for equality of opportunity he is
not greatly worried, as others are, by the meritocratic
tendencies in modern society. If his head is in the clouds
his feet are firmly on the ground.

When Husén very kindly sent me this collection of his
papers I was immediately struck by their lucidity and
elegance: many a native-born Englishman may well envy
his prose style, which bears the impress of a highly
informed and disciplined intellect. Far from being a series
of *obiter dicta,* these essays impressed me by their
coherence. Some of them have appeared as articles in
such popular North American journals as the *Saturday
Review*, while others have been published in translation
in German, Italian and other European languages. That
scarcely any of them has so far been available in English
on this side of the Atlantic seems inexcusable, and would
be quite inexplicable were it not for the provincialism
which tends to keep us preoccupied with homespun
affairs and blinkered in our modes of thought. Torsten
Husén needs no eulogy from me or anyone else: enough
to say that to introduce him to a British readership is at
once a rare pleasure and a singular privilege.

W. Kenneth Richmond

Preface

When the series of educational essays in this book were considered for publication by my English publisher, I was asked to write up some 'concluding observations'. I am not sure whether it is feasible to bring out succinctly 'conclusions' from these essays which cover such a wide array of educational topics. In a way, the essays reflect experiences which I have gained over almost a quarter of a century as an educational reformer, for a long time in my native country Sweden, and during the last decade on the international scene. Some of the chapters were originally written up in my mother tongue, others in English. Some of the major sections are revised versions of addresses given on what are regarded to be major problems in modern education. This is for example true of the introductory chapter which in the first draft existed as a farewell lecture given when I left the school of education in Stockholm after having directed its Institute of Education for almost seventeen years. Some chapters are revised articles of which a few have previously been published in various educational journals.

Since the end of the 1940s I have been closely involved in educational reform in Sweden both as a researcher and as an expert and adviser to various committees within the Ministry of Education and the National Board of Education. The central problem in Sweden, as well as in many other European countries, has been the change of the structure of the system from an élitist or selective to a comprehensive one. In retrospect I think it is fully justified to say that this has not been a purely educational or pedagogical problem, but a social and political one. I am saying this because many professional educators have during the last few decades expressed concern that politicians have 'meddled' with the affairs which have been seen as the proper realm of the educational experts. In a way, many of these experts have conceived themselves as kinds of Platonic philosopher-kings who had to tell the 'people' (including the politicians) what changes in the educational systems ought to be made (if any). The role of the politicians would then be confined to financing the plans laid down by the educators. This is, of course, to misunderstand the role of the expert. As just pointed out, the problems facing educational planners are not just problems of pedagogy. They are problems of social justice, of national economy and of preparation for a rapidly changing society where lifelong learning becomes imperative. Educational problems in a rapidly changing society are too important to be left entirely to educators. We have long since realized that military matters are too important to be left to the military!

I think it will rather soon become obvious to the reader that the author does not have a background of extensive teaching in ordinary schools or in formal teacher training. He was from the beginning a psychologist who moved into education. This is obviously a shortcoming but has also hopefully helped him to preserve the healthy aloofness to the subject and to avoid conceiving what happens in the classroom as the only important aspect of education. He has, in spite of the irritation created in the establishment, kept emphasizing that education has to be viewed in a wider social context. It does not operate in a socioeconomic vacuum. But many professional educators seem to reason as if this were the case. The present book can be seen as an attempt to provide part of the cure against such a professional disease.

During the last decade the gospel has spread that institutionalized education accounts for the major portion of economic growth. It has been asserted that education should therefore be allowed to grow more rapidly than other areas in the public sector. Society should see to it that everyone gets as much formal education as he can usefully assimilate. For a couple of decades now the majority of teenagers in Europe have gone to full-time schooling instead of working with their elders outside the school walls. I think it is time to take a critical look at institutionalized education without necessarily letting the pendulum swing to the other extreme and requiring complete 'deschooling'. I think it is of utmost importance that we try to establish our bearings now when the school as an institution seems to be on collision course with society at large.

We have to be rather ruthless in pointing out which holy cows in education we have to get rid of. I do not pretend to have conducted a systematic culling operation. Suffice it to say that some of the time-honoured conceptions have been questioned. For a 'conclusion', let me confine myself to pointing out that comparative studies of outcomes of school instruction have led me to the belief that we have grossly overemphasized the didactic aspects of education. The tricks and formal procedures in the classroom that play such an immense role in teacher training in the last analysis clearly account for only a tiny portion of the variation in learning outcomes between classrooms. If these essays focus some attention on this generality, then they will have served their purpose.

Had it not been for the enthusiasm and encouragement shown by my colleague, Professor Kenneth Richmond at the University of Glasgow, and the competent editing by my publisher, the chapters making up the present book would still have consisted of a series of scattered essays.

Torsten Husén
Institute for the Study of
International Problems in Education,
University of Stockholm.

The school and society **1**

The school as an institution: viewpoints on its present and future $\mathbf{1}$

It might seem impertinent, not to say mindless, to appear before an assembly of educators to challenge the merits of the school as an educational institution. It would be like addressing a congress of clergymen to question the competence of the Church to minister to man's religious needs. During the 100 years that have passed since public elementary education became universal in Western Europe, much of what the school does has become so institutionalized that the resultingly pronounced matter-of-course character is somehow assumed to be rooted in the metaphysical. For instance, the very structure of the school system has for a long time been assumed by many to be such that different, often parallel, school types cater for different kinds of children, who are considered to possess different types of talents and to belong to different social classes. The inculcation of knowledge and skills as set out in curricula and textbooks is supposed to be satisfactorily done only in a pretty big building (certainly in our day and age) that is divided into classrooms of about the same size. Seated in each of these rooms is a group of 20–40 pupils who are deemed capable of learning as long as they listen attentively to the preachments of one person who is called a teacher.

Since no learning is held to occur in the absence of teaching, an equals sign is interposed between learning and the activities of a licensed teacher. Thus a notion that has long prevailed widely among primary grade teachers is that parents and staff of pre-school institutions should not begin to teach children to read before they enter regular school. Primary teachers are supposed to be the best, if not the only people qualified for that task; anybody else who teaches children to read will only cause confusion.

As I pointed out, we have grown accustomed to regarding what goes on in the school as axiomatic, as something given for all time. About ten years ago I was invited to give an address at the annual meeting held by one of the Swedish national teacher associations. The topic I picked out was called, rather provokingly, 'Modes of "production" in the future school'. What I impugned in my speech was simply the time-honoured format for what is called teaching, namely to have *one* person constantly look after a group of, say, 25–40 pupils – regardless of the subject area and the objectives to be achieved by the teaching. Why not isolate the class-instruction aspect so as to have those 25–40 pupils replaced by, say 100–150? The process of one-way communication functions about equally well in both cases, or equally badly for that matter. So I went on to ask: why not get the pupils used at an early stage of schooling to working individually or in small groups instead of always operating with the same group size, the conventional class, whose appropriate size has come in for so much fruitless controversy ever since the Swedish school reforms were first debated and implemented? Then I finally asked myself: why always assign *one* teacher to a given class instead of letting the task be performed by a *team* of teachers and associates with varying degrees of experience and specialization?

These ideas, I should hasten to add, in no way originated with me. They were first formulated in the late 1950s by colleagues at the University of Chicago, where I spent a period as a visiting professor. Among the foreground figures there were Francis Chase, dean at the university's graduate school of education, and John Goodlad, later at the University of California in Los Angeles. John Goodlad launched the idea of what he called 'the ungraded school'. All that we know about individual differences conflicts with the practice, which has evolved during the past century, of dividing the pupils into grades which cover chronological age intervals. Chase actively contributed to the reorientation of educational research at American universities, the effect of which was to break its isolation by bringing all social science disciplines to bear on central educational problems. A professional disease that afflicts educators pretty much throughout the world, both out in the field and at research institutions, is to turn a blind eye to the fact that the school is and must be an integral part of the surrounding society and by no means operates in a social vacuum.

But as I said, the ideas I tried to communicate to a somewhat confused (not to mention partly shocked) audience at the 1961 teacher convention were not my own, nor were they completely new. Next day one of the pro-establishment morning newspapers ran an editorial in which I was called the 'Einstein of education', a sardonic label calculated to go down well with a dependable conservative readership. All that the editorial grasped – or perhaps wanted to grasp – was the recommendation to have classes of between 100 and 150 pupils. The newspaper ignored something else I said, namely that no more than one-quarter of school time should be spent in such groups, with the remaining three-quarters devoted to individual work and teaching in small groups.

Today, more than one decade later, various reasons are at hand that warrant a reconsideration of the problems I broached at that convention. A great deal happened during the 1960s to upset the once unshaken faith in the earlier educational order. This was the decade when sweeping school reforms pertaining to school structure and curricula were enacted in Sweden. The Education Act of 1962 abolished the system of parallel schools running from the age of eleven to sixteen and introduced all over the country a nine-year comprehensive school. This reform was implemented despite the feelings of the majority of secondary school teachers who were until then trained for a system that drew hard and fast lines between theoretical sheep and practical goats, the former earmarked for higher studies and the latter for vocational training, which for the most part meant manual trades. The education of teachers was not reformed until 1967, after many years of inquiry. Prior to the 1962 reform only one school of education, the one in Stockholm, had been in a position to furnish the Swedish school system with teachers who were trained for the new order. The upper secondary reforms of 1964 and 1969 broadened the opportunities for young people in their late teens, at the same time as a step was taken on the road towards abolishing parallelism between theoretical and practical education at the pre-university level as well.

But the 1960s also witnessed other events in the education sector in Sweden that did not attract the same attention as the structural changes and explosive enrolment increase in the teenage school. Here I chiefly allude to institutionalized adult education. Programmes of 'labour market training', i.e. the systematic retraining of gainfully employed people who because of structural changes in the economy had lost their jobs, grew from modest beginnings around 1960 to embrace more than 100,000 participants per annum by the end of the decade. In the mid-1960s, partly in consequence of the upper secondary reform and its resulting demand for 'fair shares' between the generations, the parliament voted to have the state underwrite most of the costs for a municipal programme of formal adult education which was to provide courses equivalent to those provided for the young people at both the lower and upper secondary levels. This gave many adults a chance to acquire a university training, mainly by broadening the general schooling they needed to be capable of assimilating advanced vocational training. According to a survey conducted in 1971, 154,000 persons were enrolled in municipal adult education, most of them at the upper secondary level. At the same time the publicly subsidized popular education movement, a large part of which is run by trade unions, temperance societies and similar ideological bodies, has by no means diminished in scope, even though it competes to some extent with the formal municipal programme. We must, of course, in this context not overlook the universities and professional schools. Their enrolments swelled from about 35,000 to 125,000 ten years later.

As measured by the *relative* increase of enrolment, adult education in Sweden expanded more vigorously than the teenage school during the 1960s. A great deal of evidence suggests that, to quote one wag, the teenage school has now 'had its cut'. On the assumption that new resources can be allocated to the educational system during the 1970s, priority is going to be given to adult education (and in some degree to pre-school education). We shall return to this point later.

It is quite natural that the principal weight has been attached to the greater educational opportunities that the reforms have opened up, not least for young people. The reforms of the 1950s and 1960s did not aim at major institutional changes but at realizing in the field of education the equalization already introduced in social and economic policy. Yet, in spite of all this, certain qualitative changes have been more important than the actual quantitative expansion. These changes are so significant and thoroughgoing that before long they will compel us to reappraise the very institutional forms which are basic to the school. It is therefore of the utmost importance for us to articulate *today* certain lines of thought as to how we can reform the school as an *institution,* something that we have done very little or not at all in connection with the structural reforms that were carried out during the 1960s. The handwriting is certainly on the wall, in the guise of a bitter economic reality that will soon force us to re-examine these forms from the ground up. The unit cost has gone up tremendously during the 1960s. If we now try to make planners and decision-makers conversant with new viewpoints, it may be possible to avoid current investment in things that will not be able to function in the future, thereby giving us greater scope for alternative solutions. To take one concrete example: any commitments now made to build school plants of a certain type and with fixed layouts will tie down activities inside these plants for decades ahead. An analogous case is the construction of large car parks which tend to debar alternative future solutions to traffic engineering problems in cities.

Let me try to delineate two perspectives of the present-day educational situation and school system, which to my mind are necessary to enable us to plan for tomorrow.

First of all: have we really tried to grasp the social and educational import of the fact that for the past two decades the vast majority of Swedish teenagers have been put full time into schooling rather than joining the ranks of the adult world? When I finished the six-year elementary school in 1928 to enter the municipal middle school, only one pupil out of ten went on from elementary to the next stage of non-compulsory junior secondary school. Of these youngsters rather more than half got as far as the junior secondary school certificate or entered the upper secondary school (*gymnasium*). Less than one out of every twenty 16–17 year olds at this level stayed on in full-time schooling, which was usually spent at the academic pre-university school. More than 90 per cent of the teenagers came out early in the adult society and had to assume adult roles, mainly in the job world. Today the law keeps everybody in school till the age of sixteen. But for the majority institutionalized custody continues thereafter up to the age of eighteen or nineteen.

All these figures do no more than barely hint at the *revolution* that has taken place as regards the status of youth in our society. Instead of entering the adult world to learn adult roles at the beginning of their teens, young people now find themselves in institutions where they have little or no contact with adult society until almost the end of their teens. This segregation has been reinforced by the rapid pace of urbanization: in other words, more and more children are growing up in cities and towns where their fathers – and to an increasing extent their mothers as well – spend the better part of their workday away from home. That is not the case in the countryside or rural areas, where the small business is the economic unit which dominates within the framework of the family. In consequence of the changes that have taken place, an ever larger proportion of young people are growing up without any real contact with the world of work which undoubtedly constitutes the essential part of adult existence.

The prolongation of childlike dependence on home and school to the late teens, and the problems associated therewith, have been specially accentuated by the fact that physiological puberty among today's urban youth sets in almost two years earlier than it did fifty years ago.

Second: we can obtain a perspective of events past and

present worth thinking about by going back a century to ask why the compulsory elementary school was introduced in Europe on the threshold of industrialization. Ideological reasons have often been advanced to explain this: according to the liberal school of thought, for instance, the greater measure of civic influence over public affairs required enlightened citizens, who thus needed to learn how to read and to acquire some orientation in general subjects. But isn't this explanation merely an ideological daub on the social and economic forces in western and northern Europe which compelled the emergence of a public elementary school, frequently in conflict with antipathetic farmers who wanted to keep the children at home for their productive work, work that began rather early?

As I see it, the introduction of public elementary schooling stemmed from two main causes. First, the onset of industrialism meant that the family as a production unit (we must remember that this was an agrarian and guild society in the process of change) began to break up at those places where large production units were founded with long hours of work outside the home. Parents, mostly fathers, spent a long workday at the factories. As a result the home could function less and less as the educational institution which it had so far been to some extent. These tasks had to be transferred to a separate institution which was to teach the children to read and write as well as impart certain fundamentals of the Christian faith. Industry simply needed an institution that looked after the children while it utilized the labour of their parents. Second: this labour needed to possess a basic ability to read. Some economists have concluded that during the latter half of the nineteenth century European industry needed elementary literacy among two-thirds of its work force.

We must remember that the mission of the public

elementary school of nineteenth-century Europe was to give the *common man*'s children an exceedingly limited schooling. As already indicated, this chiefly pertained to developing a modicum of skill in reading and writing plus scanty orientation to subjects of a historical and scientific nature. Perhaps the significance of this limitation will be best illustrated if we investigate how much time children in general spent in school. Compulsory attendance in, for instance, Sweden ran for six years, covering the ages from seven to thirteen. But the time that children actually spent in the building where they were taught was extremely limited well into the present century. Before 1920 full-time schooling was chiefly confined to the cities (where the minority of children were then growing up). The usual pattern in rural areas was half-time schooling or itinerant teaching. A middle-aged farmer's daughter whom I remember from my childhood home had gone to school a couple of weeks a year during the six compulsory years in the late 1880s and early 1890s. In the village where I took my elementary schooling we had a Christmas recess of two to three months because our teacher would then be holding a six-week continuation school. The summer vacation was just as long. This meant that we spent a mere half year in school for five days a week, because on Saturday the teacher had woodwork classes. In the autumn we were let out for the traditional 'potato-lifting' holiday, which had a real meaning for many of my schoolmates who came from farmer homes and had to help out at home bringing in the potato crop.

My intention with these examples has been to lend a personal touch to the basic idea behind my analysis of the school as an institution. For a long time the school's duties in nurturing the young were very limited – both in substance and in time. Until quite recently by far the most important duties relating to the socialization of young people and their induction into the activities of the larger society have fallen outside the school. Such duties involve teaching the young ones to shoulder personal responsibility and teaching them what they need to get by on their own — in short, educating them to become adults. In times past such tasks were mainly performed by the extended family, which was then a large unit. The youngsters learned adult roles in the course of interpersonal relations with parents, relatives and neighbours in the small community which was a community of work.

Today the early teens no longer signify a more or less direct transfer from the school to those adult tasks for which young people used to prepare themselves through their work with their elders in the home. They stay on in the school which has now been given, at least on paper, a broader mission with regard to imparting knowledge, and which acts as a socializing agent. We now live in a society that not only has a more complicated occupational sphere but also greater complexities of citizenship in general. The information explosion makes it more and more difficult for the individual to orient himself both inside and outside the job world. He feels that his fate lies to an ever increasing extent in the hands of experts and bureaucrats far away. One of the consequences has been to make it harder for major sectors such as manufacturing to recruit young people for direct production jobs. It simply will not do to let young people who are tired of school go out looking for jobs. Jobs are hard to find, particularly since many young people in this category come from homes that have not been highly conducive to their socialization. The big cities in Western industrial countries have a great deal of depressing experience with this category of young people. These and similar experiences have led people to the conclusion that young people should be kept in school as long as possible, even if it has to be done with legal coercion. The school is supposed to keep these low-motivated youngsters 'off the streets'. The longer the formal education they receive the better, because that will at least protect them from the misfortune of bumping their heads in vain against an unaccommodating job world. This view of how to proceed with this category of young people (who are tending to swell in numbers) is subsumed under a general viewpoint that, until quite recently, was considered self-evident, namely that every young person should in principle be given the opportunity to ingest as many years of formal schooling as he or she can swallow.

Parallel with the school's enlarged mission in terms of both substance and time, its institutional character has become strengthened. As already indicated, it is no longer responsible merely for the inculcation of certain knowledge and skills — even though these tasks have of themselves been enlarged with the advent of new subject matter. After all, there must be visible justification for the greater number of years spent in school! But the keyword in all the curricula that have been drawn up in Sweden during the past two decades is 'fostering': fostering personality, fostering responsibility, independence and co-operation. Such glamorous words have been strewn by generous hands at planning sessions and teacher seminars, and have helped to frustrate many teachers by further underlining the discrepancy between theory and bleak educational reality.

We have reached the point where it may be legitimate to subject the current school situation to some serious soul-searching. Naturally enough, those who, like me, have expounded the values and points of view which have underpinned Swedish school policy ever since the early 1950s often tend to find most of it to be excellent or nearly so; for us, that is a sort of self-defence. The shortcomings are often explained by saying that we have not yet had time to implement reforms as revolutionary as these, and that nothing is more natural than for the new which is about to emerge to be accompanied by certain throes of childbirth. A similar defence mechanism is used by politicians against young people who criticize what is going on. These young critics are in effect told that they were not around when social misery was at its worst, when unemployment was massive and when society twiddled its thumbs and did little or nothing to set matters aright.

But the attitude of 'think how much we have accomplished' which tends to prevail among the establishment turns one readily blind in the presence of today's problems. Obviously, a great deal has been accomplished in the post-war decades. Sweden has been rather successful when it comes to broadening educational opportunities, to expanding these for groups of young people who used to be shut off from advanced education. That has come about from our having gradually abolished the parallel school system, which by its structure was intended to let the lower and upper classes be served by different types of school. But have we been equally successful when it comes to achieving reforms of course content and patterns of classroom work that will make the young better prepared to shoulder adult burdens in the society of today and tomorrow? The mere fact that in different parts of the world so-called alternative schools, free schools — whatever their labels — begin to emerge is a symptom that we in the rich and highly industrialized countries have failed to create a school which stimulates young people to learn relevant things and which permits them to develop according to their individual needs. Let me accentuate that statement by saying that I am afraid that where catering for today's youth is concerned, the school is now clearly set on a collision course. It will be imperative for us to take our bearings before the collision occurs.

I believe that many people, especially among the

professional educators, are not clear in their minds about the central problem of the present-day school. They tend to locate problems almost entirely in the didactic sphere. Here I am struck by a description which was formulated by Professor James S. Coleman of the University of Chicago. He says that young people in today's urban society are shaped by an existence which is 'information rich and action poor'. In former days young people were absorbed early into an adult world that was admittedly harsh but packed with action. They had to learn early to assume responsibility, to begin supporting themselves after a few years in school, and they began at an early stage to work with adults in the home. Now they are kept outside in all these and similar respects, mainly because the adult world and the youth world are kept separate by the institutional arrangements themselves. Young people often do not know what their parents busy themselves with – indeed they have very little experience at all of what goes on in the adult world. Most of the time they find out indirectly through the mass media – and the distribution of real and pseudo events in what these communicate is of course open to debate. To all intents and purposes young people play the role of spectator, from the time they grow up when very little is done, be it in slums or suburbs, to meet their needs for activity and experience, to their teenage years in urban centres, when there is no opportunity to perform creative tasks. Much of adult life is something that contemporary youth experiences at second remove, as on a cinema screen. Very few of the young people are actively drawn into adult affairs and given an opportunity to shoulder adult responsibilities.

Unfortunately these observations also apply to the school. The reality outside the school, the real world for which the school allegedly prepares young people, is mediated by the printed and spoken word. In spite of all the fancy talk about 'self-activity' and 'learning by doing', there is no getting away from the fact that a school is a school and that its dominant attribute is to mediate reality with abstract–verbal tools. That is obviously a strength, because the abstract concepts are necessary to help us gain intellectual and technical mastery over the surrounding world. But it is also a weakness, because the abstract–verbal exercise readily become an end unto itself. The one who masters the forms, the outwork, is rewarded, while the one who can use the matter learnt is not.

The lengthening exposure to education, that is, the number of hours, weeks and years that young people spend in classrooms, together with the advent of large school plants and the intensification of central bureaucratic control that comes from standardizing textbooks, teaching aids and tests, further underlines these formalized and abstract features. The school is run as though an equals sign were interposed between teaching and learning. Learning is not assumed to take place unless the pupils listen attentively to what the teacher has to declare ; hence the many hours that go into what the officials refer to as 'creating preconditions for the conduct of teaching'. If one asks why marks are needed, the answer is that the pupils would not make an effort in their absence. Indeed, the school appears to many educators to be run in accordance with the theory of motivation which says that pupils are mainly impelled to learn in order to avoid unpleasantness. A great deal of didactics therefore builds on the assumption that pupils are fundamentally unwilling to learn anything at all, and that rewards immanent in the feeling that one has learned something relevant are immaterial in the school. From this it follows that a system must be created which makes learning the only escape hatch from various unpleasant alternatives that fence the pupil in : low marks, reproaches, complaints and so on.

Especially where the exposure to teaching is concerned, I believe that one of the most overriding problems of the present teenage school is how young people are to be given opportunities to learn meaningful things and not be deterred by the teaching to which they are exposed — for all its good intentions. The phrase 'good intentions' is well advised in this context, because it strikes me as infinitely tragic in many cases to observe the ambition that inspires the vast majority of teachers — particularly in secondary schools — and the disappointment they often feel when they cannot attract the interest of their pupils. We are then told that teaching doesn't get across because discipline is bad. A question less often asked is whether the menu offered to the pupils is to their taste. All the same, the initial motivation of the pupils must be the starting point for teaching, assuming that there is no intention to build upon the theory of education which I have just caricatured and which derives from what may be called the negative theory of motivation — the one which says that pupils undertake to learn in order to avoid unpleasantness.

When I began in the lates 1950s, partly under the influence of Coleman, to consider the meaningfulness that the school has for teenagers, I coined the term 'functional participation'. This concept has been developed in my book, *The School in a Changing Society* (Stockholm, Almqvist and Wiksell, 1961). My analyses were rooted in those studies of the school's relevance to the economy which then preoccupied the school of education (these were a research project commissioned by the 1957 Governmental School Commission). Foremen, training offices, managing directors and others engaged in the job world were interviewed to find out how well prepared young people were to assume their present duties directly after leaving school. These respondents did not complain so much about shortcomings in the knowledge and skills required for the tasks to which young people were assigned ; but they did complain at length about the lack of what may be described as 'education for work' : the ability to plan independently, to think through a problem to the end, to take initiatives and to perform tasks responsibly. Some of the respondents even went as far as to say that these young people would have to be retrained so they could behave like adults !

In the light of my earlier remarks about the information-rich but action-poor school, it is scarcely surprising that young people should in no way be prepared to shoulder adult burdens after so many years of uninterrupted schooling. Starting at the age of seven and continuing up to the age of sixteen, they have grown used to having their work planned in minute detail by the teachers hour after hour, day after day. The subject matter set out in the curriculum has been carefully prepared and dosed out in portions by ambitious educators, whose worst nightmare is that the clock will run out on them before they finish the course. The better this preparation is couched in the teaching aid itself (and after all the purport of teaching aids is to make the subject matter as easy to chew and digest as possible), the less effort and activity is required from the pupil. Those who are fired by the gospel of educational technology, if they are central bureaucrats, easily succumb to the dream that all teaching aids need only be designed with reference to goal descriptions in behavioural terms (after the docile-pupil model), and that then all education given in the country can be counted on to come under proper control. In that way, somehow, the result would be to create a central pedagogic Big Brother *à la* Orwell, who can keep detailed tabs on what the individual teachers are up to in their classrooms !

At the same time that the school, in the manner I have sought to describe, is performing its mission as an institution, namely to impart an ever swelling subject matter to more and more pupils for more and more school years, the society outside the school is undergoing changes whereby its other institutions are taking over, or are ready to take over, many of the school's time-honoured tasks in whole or in part. A few intimations should suffice here. An increasingly large part of the volume of information now available in homes is served up by newspapers and magazines. On top of that we have broadcasting. More than forty years ago I myself experienced how the radio in a rural area was becoming a more important source not only of straight news, but also of background information about events on the current scene. And then there is the more recent arrival: television. It conveys to our living rooms not only events as they unfold, but also a considerable portion of general orientation. As yet we cannot discern the end of this process. Before long we shall have the video cassette, which will provide living rooms with audiovisual communication of the material that we must now wait for together with all other viewers. The increased frequency of travel serves to broaden horizons. Lastly, we have all the contacts of an educative nature that occur in groups and organizations in contemporary society.

Life outside the school is no doubt as rich in information as that inside the school walls. This means that to the same extent that the traditional elements of learning in school are reinforced, so the conflict is exacerbated between theory and practice, between education and life. This is a conflict that teenagers, in their active search for the meaningful, experience with special intensity.

The situation I have tried to adumbrate is paradoxical indeed. At the same time that the school's classic tasks, to develop skills in reading, writing and arithmetic as well as to impart certain general knowledge, can begin to be substantially taken over by agencies outside the school, the external agencies that have looked after the actual upbringing of the young – mainly the family, the neighbourhood group or the work-at-home group – are no longer capable of giving the young what they need to prepare for entry into the adult society. At the same time that this society has become information-rich, it has also become action-poor. It is only in exceptional cases that the family can provide young people with opportunities to render contributions that are productive, can demand responsibility and instil loyalties. Such contributions are possible only in a productive working community. That sort of community is seldom to be found in today's school. It can only be achieved by performing some drastic surgery on the goals and values that govern the school, an operation that we may feel sure will not always square with the pious declarations in curricula. Typically enough the shaping of ideals among today's teenagers, as has been demonstrated by investigations both in Sweden and elsewhere, tends to be determined by peer groups more than by adults with whom the teenagers have direct contact. The peers successfully compete with the parents as setters of standards, while the teachers are caught here in a hopelessly weak position.

In a school where adults, often in the guise of abstract authorities, have predetermined, planned and prepared what is going to happen down to the last detail – even if we yet have to reach the ideal state of total control that may be envisaged by the educational technocrat – we cannot expect young people eager for action to feel at home. We cannot expect to get more independence, initiative and sense of responsibility from our young people than the school enables them to acquire.

Present-day schooling is like a mass production industry carried on in large-scale units, that is, big plants with many pupils and teachers administered by a hierarchy of bureaucrats. Production is based on the assumption that teaching and learning are highly correlated: the more teaching, the more learning. This relation is postulated to be chiefly linear, so that four hours per week return twice as much yield as two hours per week. When the 1962 Education Act increased the number of compulsory grades from seven to nine, the assumption was that the pupils would receive an equivalent increment to their knowledge. Unfortunately, investigations made on an international basis seem to show that neither the assumption of high correlation nor the one of linearity comes anywhere close to being correct. Pupils who go to school every second day or every second term for seven years appear to learn just as much as those who are in attendance every day and every term during this period. As I see it, consolation can not even be derived from believing that the latter group has been 'fostered' more than the former. Incidentally, this example can be offered as an exhibit in evidence against the frequently heard statement that educational researchers present results that all the practitioners already know, but in a language nobody understands. Actually, educational folklore abounds in myths of this kind; sad to say, they have been sacred for so long that no one is brave enough to challenge them.

At this point I should hasten to enter a qualification: no one must infer from the foregoing example that it would make no difference whether one went to school or not! Reference was made to pupils who attended school for seven years, the one group for most of the year, the other only half as long. The point is simply this: exposure to education beyond a certain level does not have the effect that we are inclined to ascribe to it. Here again the law of diminishing returns applies. Analyses of Swedish data from the International Project for the Evaluation of Educational Achievement show that low-motivated pupils even tend to lower their achievements in, for instance, science during the ninth year of their compulsory schooling.

The practical conclusions to be drawn from the

foregoing remarks – not least about the dilemma which
bedevils today's information-rich but action-poor school –
must be to make provisions for more action and thereby
turn the school into a better environment to prepare young
people for adult society. That can only be done by
eliminating or attenuating certain institutional features that
have hitherto characterized the school. In other words, the
school must be brought closer to the larger society.

Much of the effort that educators expend in their
classrooms boils down to making pupils of the pupils,
which they, I think rightly, regard as an extremely difficult
task. They complain that so much time and energy must
go into attempts to 'create preconditions for the conduct
of teaching'. As pointed out earlier, these ambitious
attempts are certainly deserving of respect. Each and every
one of us cannot avoid getting caught, as a member of the
system, in the laborious, not to say abrasive, work of
'maintaining discipline'. But at the same time one cannot
help asking whether these pains are not essentially wasted
– because discipline is not an end in itself but has to be
motivated from the tasks involved and from the types of
work that are necessary to cope with these tasks. During
the war years and the immediately ensuing period, I was
employed as a psychologist in the Swedish armed forces,
where one of my jobs was to analyse problems of military
discipline; if you think that only the school is shot
through with time-honoured institutional features, you
should have seen the army! The most remarkable excuses
were offered for holding on to disciplinary rituals that by
and by we managed to get rid of. Far be it from me to
draw a hard comparison between military service and
schooling, but there is no getting away from certain things
they have in common.

Despite all the pious talk in the curricula, the
contemporary school is marked by a high degree of formal
control, marking, individual certificate-issuing and

competition, the more so since education in present-day society has become an increasingly important highroad to careers and social status. Despite all the lip service paid to 'learning how to learn', the emphasis is put on solid knowledge, the kind that is amenable to control, measurement and marking. After all, no one can check up on the pupil to see how well he is developing his study techniques. For many years I have been emphasizing – the first time was when I submitted my brief to the 1957 Governmental School Commission – that the school's cardinal mission today is to equip pupils to cope with the information flow and not in the first place to impart solid knowledge, so called. It is therefore vital to furnish pupils with an armoury of skills that gives them this competence. But to cast doubt on the merits of content subjects – like knowing about the evolution of the horse's hoof, a problem that had me stumped when I went to lower secondary – is obviously an act of sacrilege against usage immemorial, to judge from the editorial comment on my brief published in the pro-establishment paper I mentioned earlier.

Hence the central mission of the school will be to teach the pupils to learn, to train them to assimilate new knowledge on their own. The very fact that we can no longer regard the years of childhood and youth as the exclusive preserve of education, as the years which give us all we 'need' to know for the rest of our lives, lends a tragic quixotic air to the quest to catch up with the whole course. In the information-rich society the individual has a lifelong need to educate himself, to broaden his horizons and, in many cases, to start over again. So we cannot expect the teenage school to provide a bill of fare that will nourish a whole lifetime, the more so since much of this diet does not exist during the pupil's years in school but will be produced at different stations along the road.

The latter-day discussion about so-called recurrent

education, sponsored by the OECD and essentially inspired from Sweden, is an interesting sign of the times. The educational policymakers have begun to ask themselves whether a defensible case can be made for encouraging young people to spend for ever and a day on full-time education. One reason this question has been brought up, and of course it is one to which politicians are highly sensitive, is the tremendously escalating cost of education – an expenditure that industrial countries like Sweden find increasingly hard to finance. There are grounds for expecting that the steeply rising expenditure per pupil and year will soon compel drastic measures, for instance with regard to the volume of teacher-guided instruction, but also with regard to the feasibility of letting everybody attend school full-time up to the age of twenty. Many signs indicate that we shall soon have a system where periods of gainful employment will alternate with schooling after a certain age is reached, say from sixteen to eighteen. If we deem it a realistic future perspective for about 15 per cent of life after the age of twenty to be devoted to further education, training and retraining, it will not be so important for the individual to stay in school full-time right up to the age of eighteen to twenty.

It goes without saying that the idea of recurrent education is not mainly inspired by financial motives. We have an overriding social motive for it, namely that in a continuously changing society it simply will not do to prepare for the whole life we shall have inside and outside the job world, for the reason that the years of youth come under the jurisdiction of a society whose demands and conditions differ from those of adulthood. The process of change constantly requires further education and reorientation. On top of that comes a 'fair shares' motive, which is to say that a person should not miss out on the chance to benefit from quality education if he did not receive it, or did not care for it, when he was young. When an individual is enabled to re-enter the system any time he feels like it, and this is happening for instance in programmes of adult education, there will be better potential for creating greater equality of educational opportunity between the generations and between different groups in the same generation.

I have brought up the topic of recurrent education because it is sure to have repercussions on the school, mainly in that it can be expected to break the institutional isolation and bring theory and practice, learning and life, closer to one another.

What changes can be expected in the school as an institution during the next few decades? As I see it, the school faces two main alternative futures. The one is that its Byzantine isolation from society will continue, which can have but one outcome: the school will perish in an Armageddon, and from its ashes completely new types of education may grow. The second alternative is a transformation by degrees. This transformation must take place in two essential respects. My remarks below represent conclusions from the analysis performed above.

First of all: the school must be able to give teenagers the opportunity to take part in meaningful tasks where they are made to feel productive in the broad sense and to play pertinent roles in the adult community. We must give them the opportunity to acquire a growing responsibility for tasks which affect the welfare of their fellow humans. By rendering contributions to the adult community and being treated as adults, they will learn the adult roles.

Over a period of some years in Sweden we have had so-called practical vocational guidance in terms of a few weeks of work experience in the upper grades of the comprehensive school. But this is a brief orientation that can furnish no more than a taste of the conditions and demands imposed by the job world. We would have to let *all* young people experience for a longer period, say after the age of sixteen, what it means to shoulder the discipline that comes from sharing with others the responsibility for carrying out major tasks. This can hardly be done – and we might as well look matters straight in the face – under the individualistic auspices of competition and marks that characterize today's school.

Efforts should be made to investigate at length the extent to which it would be possible to let the vast majority of young people enter the job world for longer periods – to give them training for responsibility and the much-needed opportunity to grow into adult roles. For instance, what about permitting young people to practise in certain rapidly expanding and highly labour-intensive service occupations, such as child welfare, sick care and old-age care? This would enable them to render contributions which, while admittedly modest in absolute terms, are still highly meaningful. Such practical experience would put the youngsters in greater touch with people of other generations. They would get to learn about such things as the problems of ageing, of patients in hospitals, of gainfully employed mothers and so on. In that way they would also find relevant use for the social and psychological knowledge picked up in classrooms and textbooks.

We could also let older pupils have a go at teaching their younger schoolmates. The experiments made in this field have proved so encouraging as to warrant their continuance. One of their by-products would be to provide the personal guidance that is needed to make teaching more individualized.

It is in this connection also that one should view pupils' contributions to decision-making. This is an issue that has come up during the past few years in the somewhat confused debate on school democracy and pupil participation. It has often been regarded as a matter of bringing influence to bear on the decision process or, if you like, a question of who is to exercise power. To my mind, the essential aspect is to create a work environment which enables pupils to feel a functional participation, and thus helps teach them to plan, to assume responsibility and impose on themselves discipline for common tasks. Anyone who is not *permitted* to assumed responsibility will not impose any discipline upon himself but will have it imposed on him by others. Hence the issue of pupil participation does not mainly boil down to the actual forms of decision-making in the school, but rather to the institutional forms as a whole: in other words, whether the school is to remain an institution of the kind it now is.

Second: the school must try to exploit the wealth of information that exists in other public agencies and institutions and turn it to useful account. As a matter of course we shall also have enduring need of professionally trained educators – teachers – at all levels. But the important thing is for the school to take systematic advantage of the competence and expertise to be found outside the school. Journalists, writers, politicians (not least in local government) and eminent professionals in general comprise an enormous untapped reservoir of talent that could well be put to use in the school, many among them not only intermittently but also for sustained periods. For that matter, why stop there? Would not the educators themselves also benefit from the opportunity to alternate between classrooms and other workplaces, the better to see themselves in perspective as educators? Theirs is an occupation that invites more than most others the risk of isolation and inbreeding.

For natural reasons an attempt such as this, with its sweeping, visionary reflections, is bound to be categorical and schematic. Some of the subject matter covered will no doubt be regarded as a pretentious exercise in audacity. I do by no means belong to those who want to blow up the school or to 'deschool' society. But the mere fact that the very worthwhileness of the school as an institution has come under debate is an indication that its compatibility with conditions prevailing in the affluent, highly industrialized and service-oriented modern society is questionable. The purpose of setting forth the points of view above has been to get across the message that it is time to begin to cast a critical eye on the school as an institution. The outcome of such a critical examination would hopefully be solutions which would avoid the extremes, be they either further bureaucratic formalism and institutionalization or a 'deschooling' that would mean a 'return to nature' which is impossible in a technological society.

Individual differences and individualized instruction

'The flunkers are always with us'

By longstanding tradition the type of instruction conducted in that institution which goes under the name of school has built upon three assumptions, which as a rule are perceived to be axiomatically self-evident:

(1) Pupils undertake to learn mainly to avoid the disagreeable consequences if they do not: low marks, non-promotion, censure, punishment, etc.
(2) Some pupils 'get through' an assigned quantum of learning and others do not, mainly because the former have more so-called scholastic ability. Some pupils are simply *bound* to fail when they tackle such subjects as algebra, a foreign language or nuclear physics.
(3) Ability is chiefly manifested in the successful performance of increasingly complex tasks of the type which confront the pupil in school and/or in textbooks. The more complex the tasks he copes with, the greater his ability.

These assumptions have generated important consequences for the school and the instruction it gives.

First of all, judgements must be passed in the form of marks and non-promotion, for otherwise many pupils would lose their incentive to learn. It cannot be assumed that they will learn chiefly because a particular subject or task in hand will of itself stimulate interest; in other words, the only way to get the pupils to ingest the assigned lesson is to hang a proper sequence of swords of Damocles over their heads.

Second, it is more or less given by nature for a certain number of pupils to fail at a given stage in a given subject, just as surely as there will be a certain proportion who are destined to succeed. Therefore it stands to reason that there should be a system of absolute marks with specified lower limits or so-called passmarks. This has often been taken as virtually metaphysically anchored. At all events, the relative proportions of those who pass and fail in a certain type of school exhibit over a long time-span a marvellous constancy, notwithstanding the variable numbers of a cohort who go through the system.

In France it was long part of the tradition for about half the students who sat for the baccalaureate or final secondary school examination to fail – this in spite of the fact that admissions to the *lycée* were screened and the usual quota of non-promotions occurred as the students moved up through the grades. Research on examinations (*docimologie*) had proved that the average correlation between two independent examiners unknown to one another did not appreciably deviate from chance, i.e. from zero, but these findings could not dislodge the examination system for many years. Although never stated explicitly, it was somehow thought useful or stimulating to flunk from 40 to 50 per cent of the candidates in each separate section of the examination.

Examples of a similar state of affairs can be cited for Sweden. The 1940 Royal Commission on schools made a thorough inquiry into the route travelled by pupils through the lower secondary academic school (*realskola*). By and large, it was found that two out of every three starters reached the point of qualifying for admission to the *gymnasium* or pre-university school. One out of every two completed the course without having to repeat a grade. These findings pertained to conditions in the late 1930s and early 1940s, when roughly one-sixth of every cohort went to lower secondary academic school or its equivalent. Analogous inquiries were made by the 1957 Governmental School Commission, which followed up a random sample consisting of every fifth pupil admitted in 1953. Notwithstanding the fact that admissions had increased to the point where between one in two and one in three elementary pupils went to lower secondary academic school, it was found that the percentages of non-promotions and drop-outs held at the same levels.

The practical consequence of the third assumption, where scholastic ability is supposed to manifest itself by successful performance on increasingly complex tasks, is that certain tasks are by 'nature' such that no more than a handful of pupils can master them. If the teacher tries to explain, say, a mathematical theorem, he must anticipate that only a limited – and given – number of pupils will have any inkling of what it is all about.

Anyone who has had experience of designing so-called intelligence tests knows that the object is to increase the degree of difficulty by such devices as making the word choices more esoteric or by drawing 'decision trees' with more and more ramifications. Class instruction of the traditional type and standardized tests both produce 'normal distributions' of performance, with the great majority of pupils clustering round the mean and continually diminishing frequencies in the direction of both extremes. Inasmuch as certain biological variables, e.g. standing height, are also normally distributed, the conviction has long prevailed that school performances are destined by some God-given rule to follow the same Gaussian curve.

Thinking anew didactically

A question asked not only by far-seeing educational thinkers but also by experimenters with vision is: why not put motivation into the actual subject matter a pupil works with and is supposed to learn? Why should learning in the school be chiefly controlled by extrinsic motivation, whereas the rest of life essentially builds upon intrinsic motivation? Skinner gave a malicious twist to this in one of his early writings on programmed instruction, where he said in effect: an American student of French who can say flawlessly 'Please pass me the salt' gets a high mark – whereas in France he will actually be given the salt! Obviously it should not be expected that everything the school tries to inculcate, even when concocted in tasty morsels and with fancy dressing, can be responded to with an original interest, for which reason there must be certain extrinsic influences in the form of, say, praise and censure. But many pupils are unable to cope with some tasks even with the best intrinsic motivation, and hence they are bound to perceive extrinsic spurs – such as periodically given marks – as incessant punishment. The greatest possible provision ought to be made instead for 'embedding' these tasks in contexts that encourage the pupil to feel he is making progress as he is enabled to master them more effectively.

A decade or so ago some eminent American experimental psychologists began to devote themselves to fundamental educational issues. One of them was Jerome Bruner of Harvard University. He took a special interest in cognitive learning, with emphasis on how a body of subject matter should be presented in order to be appropriately assimilated.

In the introduction to his book *On Knowing*, he made the provocative statement that there is no subject matter which a pupil cannot learn by intellectually honourable means, regardless of his age. Accordingly, the educational problem is not *if* a pupil can learn, but rather *how* he is to learn. Bruner thereby tackled one of the sacred didactic cows, namely the one embodying the assumptions that subject matter must be grouped by age in certain ways and that some things cannot be learned by pupils before they reach a certain age. The organization of the 'new mathematics' is usually cited as an example of the revolution triggered off by Bruner's line of thinking. Thus it was long held that the theory of numbers was so difficult and complicated that not even the *gymnasium*'s science curriculum could find a place for it. With the new disposition of courses devised by, among others, Beberman and his associates, the theory of numbers is already taught in the first year of basic school. This also serves to exemplify a change of thinking that has taken place in curriculum-building circles, namely that the pupils must not learn a subject as traditionally planned by method specialists and textbook authors, but should be enabled to learn it as a discipline. Where mathematics is concerned, for example, the theory of numbers already comes in from the beginning. To teach a subject as a discipline necessarily entails pupils being given the greatest possible opportunity to learn by 'insight' rather than by rote. Penetration of a field of human knowledge through insight, and with the help of a methodology that gives at least some consideration to how creative researchers went about making their fundamental discoveries, ought to be a better stimulus of motivation than methods which assume that the subject is given, that the truths are already explained, and that it is the pupil's duty to swear to the schoolmaster's words and above all to learn these.

Causes of varying school performance

Studies undertaken in the past few years, drawing in part on the theory of classroom learning formulated by John B. Carroll, have sought to identify the causes of variability in the learning performances of pupils, with particular reference to what makes these performances 'normally distributed'. Alongside differences of ability and personality, varying performances in school as reflected by the 'normal' distribution and other statistical representations are conditioned by two circumstances.

Every teacher holds an *expectation* that a certain and often rather limited number of pupils will be able to learn what the syllabus 'prescribes' within the allotted time (or what the textbook has arbitrarily defined as the prescribed subject matter). He also holds the expectation that some pupils will be unable to cope and must therefore be flunked. These expectations are transmitted to the pupils in ways that are often subtle and seldom explicit. Some of the pupils, especially if they have a 'school-motivated' background, will soon perceive themselves as destined to succeed, while others will perceive the opposite. One is reminded of what social psychologists call the 'self-fulfilling prophecy', the tendency of a person to live up to the expectations that others have of him.

Obviously self-assessments of success and failure depend not only on the existing expectations but also on comparisons of actual performances in the classroom. However, these standards of assessment are bound to be rather localized, i.e. based on what a pupil sees in his own class or at most in his own school. The research team under Professor Benjamin Bloom in Chicago, which studied the complex of problems intertwined with individualized learning and teaching, investigated two classes who differed so much from one another in their performances that the resulting distributions did not overlap at all: the best pupil in the poor class did not come up to the worst pupil in the best class. It was found that the former pupil felt he had done very well by himself, whereas the later pupil considered himself a failure.

There is also a great deal of evidence to suggest that expectations as to how many are going to 'pass' a certain examination or test helps to make the distribution what it is. The expectations certainly serve to broaden the variability, in that some are spurred by the prospect of doing well, while others are dejected before they start by being regarded as potential failures.

The second essential factor which shapes the distribution of scholastic performance is the degree of *individualization* with regard to time and method or, more accurately, the extent to which instructional individualization is lacking. According to studies based on Carroll's theoretical model of classroom learning, the individualization of both time and methodology, inclusive of textbooks and other teaching aids, can greatly reduce the spread of final performances and at the same time considerably raise the average. It is reasonable to expect that ordinary classroom teaching or 'frontal instruction', which theoretically exposes all pupils to essentially the same pedagogical stimuli for equally long periods, inevitably entails a considerable time spread in the learning process. Some pupils are capable of assimilating the instruction and of attaining the standard which the teacher demands. Others are quite incapable for the simple reason that they need much more time and more individualized aids, with the result that they lag more or less behind.

Carroll first presented his model in an article published by *Teachers College Record* in 1963. The model has since then been subjected to empirical testing by himself and other researchers. He himself tried it out as part of an IEA research project on the learning of foreign languages. Benjamin Bloom of Chicago University has directed a research group which conducted studies in a number of schools.

It would take us too far afield to elaborate on Carroll's model in the present context. Suffice it here to call attention to its seminal ideas. The 'strategic' factor in his theory is time, and the time needed to learn something in a specific subject or subject area is determined by aptitude. In an experiment designed by the Chicago group, the pupils were called upon to practise various exercises, e.g. learning a series of German word lists or deriving a theorem. The same pupils were given Thurstone's test of primary mental abilities. Their scores on this test were correlated with the times needed to master the different exercises. It turned out that the time taken to learn the German word lists correlated very highly with the test score for verbal aptitude and memory. In other words, the difference of learning ability as measured by time are largely explained by differences of primary mental ability. Hence time would appear to be the 'strategic' factor in the sense which Carroll means.

Obviously the time required for learning can explain the variability of school performances only in part, though it is admittedly an important factor in that it may explain half or more of the differences. But the following factors are also important. One is the quality of instruction, construed in terms of how thoroughly the teacher explains the problems or of his ability to make specific allowance for individual differences. Further, it definitely cannot be taken for granted that every pupil actually receives the time he needs to learn the prescribed subject matter. A great deal of learning is bound to be interrupted before a pupil reaches the stage of mastery. Irrespective of the quality of teaching and the time allotted to the pupils, they are unlike in their ability to comprehend the presentation, both of the teacher and the aids used. The pupils are also unlike in their perseverance : some are less motivated than others and hence less disposed to keep trying.

What consequences do these observations have for the planning of instruction and the treatment of pupils?

Individualization of methods and teaching aids

The principles that have traditionally governed the grading of school performance must be reappraised in the light of the experiences quoted above. A marking system whose main import is to compare a pupil with his coevals, either with those who sit in the same classroom and/or those who belong to the same grade throughout the country, serves to instil in some a permanent sense of failure, with all that this implies for motivation. What the individual pupil needs to know (and his teacher, too) is whether his performance curve is moving up or down. In other words, he needs first of all to be compared with himself. That is one of the ways in which the school can give all its pupils the opportunity to experience success. The marking system in many countries used up to the present time stems from the early nineteenth century, a period when social mobility increased in the wake of the French Revolution and when the academic school viewed its chief task as the competitive screening of a social and/or intellectual élite for leading positions in society. Society has since then become more 'meritocratic' in the sense that education has increasingly become an instrument for improving social status. But today there is no longer the question of safeguarding the emergence of a small élite. An ever larger proportion of the cohort is now supposed to be enabled to reach the level that was formerly thought attainable by no more than a small minority. Nor is education over with the end of formal schooling. In the 'learning society' of our time it is a lifelong process. It then becomes important to implant in all pupils a 'taste for more' so that a significant number do not drop out with a feeling of frustration and failure.

Everything must be done to organize school work along lines that permit learning at individually set speeds and let the method of class instruction die a slow death. For that to take place, two essential conditions must be fulfilled : adequate teaching equipment, preferably of the self-instructive type with graduated difficulty levels, must be produced, and provision made for teacher training that responds to this methodology. Within another decade or so it should be possible to reckon with the full-scale operation of material-methods systems for the majority of skill subjects and perhaps also for some content subjects.

However, it is not enough to organize the work so that the pupils can, in principle, be kept going with a given subject matter until the majority have learned it adequately. It is also necessary to vary the types of instruction and the auxiliary facilities in ways that help every pupil to learn with the strategy which suits him best. I should like to call that the individualization of methods and teaching aids. Such individualization ought to take hold in the very first year of school for dealing with the basic skills of reading and writing. A classroom I visited at the college of education at the University of Hawaii, containing about thirty pupils between 5 and 7 years old, featured some half-dozen different types of equipment for programmed and individualized training, including a programmed electric typewriter, a cassette projector to demonstrate the writing down of letters and words, material for practising phonics, and so on.

Of the preliminary findings made by the Chicago group, perhaps the most interesting is the dependence of learning outcomes on method. As noted earlier, it was found that the time needed to learn a particular lesson, e.g. a theorem, was highly correlated with different combinations of primary abilities. However, the combinations which correlate with time expenditure vary according to the didactic alternatives used in the lessons and the aids available to the pupils. Thus exclusive class instruction based essentially on the textbook is highly correlated with verbal ability and memory, whereas methodically varied instruction which aims at the grasp of relationships tends to correlate highly with logical ability and 'creativity'. In their book on creativity and intelligence in the school, Getzels and Jackson of Chicago showed that the conventional classroom methods tend to produce learning outcomes whose correlation with the so-called intelligence test is fairly high, but with creativity tests is low. Thus the 'cognitive style' of the instruction, apart from giving certain material information, also has the formal effect of shaping the intellectual instruments of the pupils, i.e. the ways in which they acquire and assimilate knowledge in the first place.

We have crossed the threshold of the 'learning society'. It is a society that calls for lifelong mass education: where this was once the prerogative of a highly limited élite, it must now be dispersed more broadly, especially at the secondary and university levels. Accordingly, the conviction of an earlier day that only a few can 'succeed' and 'go far' in the system amounts to a serious handicap, the more so since it does not square with a 'properly' organized reality.

3   What is an 'achievement standard'?

'Standard' is an old notion in pedagogical folklore. Every time the question of broadening educational opportunities has arisen, quite a lot of experts have rushed to the scene with forebodings of 'lowered standards'. If a study of Swedish educational history in the twentieth century has anything to teach us — and I suspect that the same applies to other European countries — it is that every change of the system towards the kind of school organization and curricula we have today has been accompanied by these Jeremian prophecies. From time to time I have amused myself by asking people what they really mean when they use the word 'standard'. The answers have ranged from total muteness to 'Well, everybody knows that.' When I have persisted with some of them, they come up with either of two definitions: it refers to the average level of achievement or to the minimum pass requirements a school sets up for its pupils.

When the revised curriculum for the Swedish comprehensive school was proposed by the National Board of Education in 1967, the editorial columns of some Swedish newspapers began to pontificate on 'lowering the achievement level' and 'achievement standards in the comprehensive school'. Since readers could be excused for not knowing what these concepts meant (the editorialists did not seem to know, either) some straightening out may be in order.

As I see it, the term 'standard' can be given a rational meaning in two respects. First, it relates to the educational objectives sought for a specific type of school in accordance with the given curriculum. These objectives can be expressed not only with generally worded criteria on cognitive or non-cognitive goals, but may also be made operational in principle, i.e. expressed as concrete achievements and behaviour. Second, the ability of a given school type to live up to its objectives may be expressed with the help of descriptive statistics. It is not self-evident which statistical measure ought to be used. I shall briefly mention some alternative measures that with varying degrees of completeness reflect the quality of an educational system.

As implied above, many educators perceive 'standard' to be something absolute, an almost metaphysically given level of achievement a pupil must attain to get his 'pass' and/or qualify for promotion to the next grade or stage. This perception was fairly common in the earlier lower secondary academic school (*realskola*) in Sweden and is common in today's German *gymnasium* still and in the French *lycée*. It signifies that a pupil is mainly judged by whether or not he has scraped past the absolute standard limit, not by his relative position on a scale of achievements.

'Standard' may also be expressed in relative terms, i.e. by comparing one individual or a group of individuals with the distribution of achievement in a reference population. The term is used in this sense with reference to the 'standard tests' that have been used in the Swedish compulsory schools since the mid-1940s in order to establish between-school equivalence of marking.

In so far as a minimum of articulation has obtained in educational thinking, standards have been rated by comparing average achievements. It has been found, for example, that the average pupil in the former secondary academic school scores much higher in mathematics than his comprehensive school coeval, or that American 18 year olds show a considerably lower average than Britons of the same age.

At this point the difficulties of making meaningful comparisons between different educational systems or school types begin to make themselves known. First of all, a standard is supposed to be gauged in relation to the stated objectives. This is by way of saying that the tests used to measure objectives must be reasonably representative so as not to favour any one type of school unduly. In other words, a comparison between the academic secondary school and the comprehensive school must employ methods that take existing differences of objectives into account. To say out of hand that the comprehensive school gives a lower achievement level than the academic secondary is the same as saying that the former must emulate the latter in its objectives and course content.

The really big difficulty of comparison, however, does not lie with methods that give each set of objectives a fair deal. In spite of everything, the common core of knowledge and skills is usually greater than might be expected from the different ways in which objectives are formulated in the curricula for different school types. As soon as an attained 'standard' has to be evaluated, another and more essential comparability problem interposes itself, namely the practice of indiscriminately comparing groups which comprise very different proportions of the same age category. If we compare the achievement standard in, say, mathematics of 18 year olds in the senior class of an American high school with that of their coevals who sit for the general certificate of education (GCE) in Britain or its equivalent in the Federal Republic of Germany (the *Oberprimaner*), the American average turns out to be way below the European. The pointlessness of this exercise stands out when we discover that 75 per cent of the age cohort in the United States is compared with 10 to 20 per cent of that in Germany or Britain. All it does, actually, is to relate the performance of a vast majority in one place with that of a carefully screened élite in another. If finding out what a limited group of pupils (most often selected not only by intellectual but also by social criteria) achieves is to make sense, then in all fairness the comparison should relate to *equal shares* of the cohorts. That was done for the international evaluation of mathematics instruction, where countries were compared with reference to the top 4 per cent of pupils in the final grade of the pre-university school. The intercountry differences then proved to be relatively small. Thus it was found that the top 4 per cent in the US, where the great majority in this grade attained an achievement only half as high as their European coevals, nevertheless lie on about the same level with them. In other words: there was an élite in the subject even for a system that does not mainly aim at producing an élite.

However, the question of what standard a school system attains does not only apply to the pupils it keeps but also to those who for various reasons drop out – or who are not admitted in the first place. This involves, among other things, the price, as measured by exclusions and drop-outs, that is paid for the quality of those who survive the system. Let me illustrate the problem with reference to non-promotions and failures in the German *gymnasium*. Out of 100 pupils, who are admitted after careful screening, about twenty sit for their final examinations after the 'normal' time lapse, i.e. without having repeated a grade. The greater number will have left school before then, usually because of non-promotion. It stands to reason that such a price must enter into a calculus of the standard attained by a specific type of school.

Different school systems have varying degrees of 'retentivity', i.e. they differ with regard to the proportion of the age cohort which is still in school at a given age level. As we have seen, the United States ranks high on this count. It is also high in Japan, where up to 65 per cent of the 18 year olds are in full-time schooling. Sweden has during the last fifteen years greatly increased its retentivity through its school reform. The same holds true for some Eastern European countries. East Germany, for instance, has a higher retentivity than West Germany. A meaningful evaluation of the standard must therefore seek answers to the question 'how many have been carried on how far?' and not only to 'how far along have the best come?' The first question bears crucially on gauging not only the extent to which an educational system is democratic in that it gives opportunities to all, but also to what extent it is adapted to a society and an economy it is meant to serve. The society which predominates in the industrially advanced countries requires élites of a quite different character from in the past. In the first place everyone needs a much better education than used to be the lot of the common man. To that extent the vast majority will soon become an élite by comparison with earlier generations. Not only that, but there is no longer need for an extremely limited group of practitioners at the professional level. At that level the economy of a future society will require something that approaches mass education.

Evidently, it cannot be expected that young people in the Sweden of the 1980s, when well over 25 per cent will be undergraduates in higher education, will reach the same high 'standard', i.e. average achievement, as the 3 per cent who were undergraduates thirty years earlier. The interesting comparison, however, is whether the very best among that one-quarter will be just as good as the one-thirtieth of their predecessors who went to university. Nor will it be uninteresting to find out how the remaining undergraduates of the 1980s will compare with the majority of youngsters back in the 1940s who ended their formal education after seven years of elementary school.

Does amount of instruction make a difference?

During the latter part of the 1950s the Institute of Educational Research at the school of education in Stockholm conducted a five-year evaluation study of the relative 'efficacy' of selective and comprehensive types of school. The findings were reported by one of my co-workers, Dr Nils-Eric Svensson, in a monograph entitled *Ability Grouping and Scholastic Achievement* (Stockholm, Almqvist & Wiksell, 1962). When social background and IQ were allowed for, the outcomes of instruction in the various types of school structure in grades 5 to 9 turned out to be very much the same. I remember that when I told this to Professor Francis S. Chase, at that time dean of the graduate school of education at the University of Chicago, he answered jokingly, 'Well, that does not surprise me. It fits wonderfully my hypothesis that schooling doesn't make much difference!'

It has been part of the traditional creed of education that selectivity both in terms of admission and promotion is to the advantage of both bright and dull students. Another notion anchored even more firmly in educational belief has been that there is a linear relationship between amount of exposure to instruction and retained knowledge. In both cases it is taken for granted that the institutional type of formal schooling accounts for the major part, if not the entirety, of knowledge and skills imparted to young people. Thus in order to improve standards one has to increase the number of years of schooling and/or the number of hours a subject is taught per week.

In a country with a national curriculum, subject areas and hours per week are determined by the parliament because this is an important factor in determining appropriations. In these circumstances competition between spokesmen for the various subject areas can be rather fierce. I still remember vividly the battle over hours per week fought inside and outside the Swedish National Board of Education when the upper secondary school curriculum was revised. Action was taken by various pressure groups who tried to influence the government to submit a secondary school bill to the parliament which would favour their respective interests. It was contended that a reduction by only one period of the time allotted to mathematics would impair the competitive strength of Sweden in the world market and that a similar reduction of teaching time for biology would likewise endanger the quality of medical education. Not to mention that a reduced timetable for Latin would herald a cultural twilight in our country.

All countries with some kind of basic, compulsory schooling have regulations specifying the age at which children have to enter school. This varies quite a lot. In countries with rather developed systems of schooling the age range tends to be five to seven. In England, for instance, children enter at five, whereas in Scandinavia they do not start school until seven. In most other developed countries the normal age of entry is six. One striking feature of the school system in the developing countries is the highly flexible age of entry. Together with the high rate of repetition this accounts for the large age spread in elementary schools in these countries.

Prior to the massive survey studies which were launched during the 1960s by the International Association for the Evaluation of Educational Achievement (IEA), cross-national studies which set out to elucidate the effects of age of school entry were rather scarce. There were a few investigations comparing attainments of British, American and Australian children in the three Rs. In most cases these studies had a common language. D. A. Pidgeon, for instance, found that English children at seven, ten and fourteen years of age tended to perform better than Californian children. In most cases national random samples were not drawn which, of course, impaired the representativeness of the data collected and made conclusions very difficult. Furthermore, it was extremely difficult to sort out to what extent age of school entry (which as a rule varied by only one year) contributed to the observed differences, in comparison to the quality of instruction and the standard set for it.

The effect of the age of school entry was one of the problems studied by the IEA on the basis of testing representative samples of 13 year olds in twelve developed countries. It was stated in the main report (published in 1967 under my editorship) that the 'results suggest, but do not establish beyond doubt, that school systems admitting pupils at the age of 6 produce mathematics scores at the age of 14 which are superior to those obtained by students in systems admitting children at 5 or delaying admission to 7' (p. 68). It should, however, be pointed out that among the countries included in the study, entry at the age of five occurred only in England and Scotland and at seven only in Sweden and Finland. The remaining eight countries had an entry at six. One cannot of course generalize on the basis of observations from so few systems. Nevertheless, assuming that it is possible to keep other sources of variation in achievement under control, the mere fact that earlier entry does not seem to bear any substantial relationship to achievement at the age of thirteen ought to cast some doubt upon the proposition that the earlier the children are brought to school the earlier they can leave it. A corollary to this is that the labour market would thereby be provided with one or more age cohorts of productive citizens. T. N. Postlethwaite reanalysed the mathematics data and came out with the conclusion that school entry at five did not seem to 'be of consequence as far as progress in mathematics is concerned, whereas a loss of a year's schooling between six and seven appears to have a detrimental effect' (*School Organization and Student Achievement*) (Stockholm, Almqvist & Wiksell, 1967). Furthermore his findings suggested that earlier entry was correlated with later progress more among children with a white collar than among those with a blue collar background. Similar analyses concerning age of entry to school and comprising data from twenty countries both for 10 year old and 14 year old students were published in 1973. At the same time the amount of pre-schooling in the respective countries was also considered.

By and large we assume that exposure to teaching is highly related to student learning and in a linear fashion — that is to say, that an increase in full-time schooling from, for instance, six to nine years would result in an increase of imparted knowledge by some 50 per cent. In my opinion pedagogical folklore of this type alone could account for the fierce battles over timetables mentioned above. The desire among subject matter specialists to build up their own empires hopefully plays only a secondary role in this context.

So far only very limited empirical evidence has become available to serve as a knowledge base for those who prepare and decide about timetables. These are in many cases decided upon by the national government or state parliament, which means that they tend to be uniform within the respective countries. Studies of how instruction time in a particular subject area is related to achievement would therefore have to be cross-national, or more precisely, multi-national. Certain leads, can, however, be obtained from national surveys in which students in all subjects have been assigned widely different amounts of instruction time.

In sparsely populated areas in Scandinavia it was earlier the normal practice, due either to teacher shortage or to the school being a long distance away, to allow children to go to school every other semester or every other day during part of even all of their compulsory school period. In the 1950s Mogstad conducted a survey in a rural region of Norway in which two parallel groups of students from twelve to fourteen were taught full-time and half-time respectively during the last two grades of compulsory school. The second group, which was assigned more homework, turned out to be only slightly inferior to the first in terms of basic skills. Similar evidence has been collected in Sweden, where since the middle of the 1940s achievement tests in the three Rs have been administered to all students at certain grade levels.

So far, the IEA six-subject survey is the only comprehensive multi-national attempt to relate number of hours of instruction to retained skills and knowledge as measured by international achievement tests. From the methodological point of view, the thorny problem is to relate the amount of exposure to formal teaching to achievement, when differences in other conditions which are also related to achievement, such as parental education, rural–urban domicile and teacher competence, are accounted for. I shall confine myself here to some of the findings of the IEA mathematics survey. We are now in the midst of reporting the data for an additional six subjects in twenty countries, among them four less developed ones. It would, however, be somewhat premature to present findings from this later phase of the IEA survey work. Suffice it to mention here that I have so far not discovered anything that strongly contradicts the conclusions arrived at in the mathematics survey on the instruction time issue.

In the IEA mathematics study an attempt was made by means of regression analyses to find out to what extent differences between students within the twelve countries were accounted for by home background, and by teacher, school and student variables respectively. Among supposedly important groups of school variables were 'length of the school week', 'the time given to all homework', 'the time given to mathematics homework' and 'the time given to instruction in mathematics'. Together these accounted for only about 3 per cent of the total variance on the mathematics test among the 13 year olds. It should, however, be kept in mind that on average only one-third of the total variance was absorbed by the twenty-six factors which went into the analysis. A better measure of the relative importance of the four time factors which described learning is obtained by saying that they together absorb only 10 per cent of the assignable variance.

Of the four factors under scrutiny here, 'time given to all homework' tended to be the important one for the 13 year olds (when 100 per cent of the age cohort were still in full-time schooling), whereas 'time given to mathematics homework' and 'time given to instruction in mathematics' (in that order) were the important ones at the pre-university level. Thus at both levels instruction time seemed to be close to insignificant in all the twelve countries included in the study.

The number of hours of instruction of students studying mathematics at the pre-university level varied from an average of 4·3 hours (lowest country) to 8·9 hours (highest country). Amount of instruction did not seem to bear any significant relationship to the performance on the mathematics test. The rank order correlation over countries was only +0·13. It should, however, be pointed out that the number of hours of instruction during the current school year is not a satisfactory measure of the amount of exposure to instruction. When analysing the data for Australia in the IEA mathematics study Dr John Keeves used the total time spent on learning mathematics at school up to the age of thirteen (during seven years). This differed considerably, in contrast to the time spent during the current year, between the states. Keeves found that the total time of mathematics teaching was significantly related to the average performance on the mathematics tests for the five Australian states.

The findings cited above – and these will admittedly be suggestive rather than conclusive until the six-subject survey has been completed – have important policy implications both for developed and developing countries. The latter nations tend to rely on institutional patterns set by the wealthy, industrialized countries in their attempts to modernize their own education. Universal elementary schooling for the masses in Western Europe was introduced in a half-industrialized society where parents had long working hours in factories and where the home was less and less able to serve as the training ground it had been previously, when members of the family spent the whole day producing and consuming together. Apart from providing children with some basic skills in the three Rs and some knowledge in the Scriptures, the school also fulfilled a custodial task. Industry simply needed an institution that could look after the children while it utilized their parents' labour. The high rate of wastage in terms of grade-repeating and drop-out as well as a salary structure which makes schooling relatively more expensive in the developing countries casts some doubt upon the worthwhileness for these countries of the institutional model taken over from Europe and the United States. The fact that staff salaries account for two-thirds of the operating costs of schools, perhaps even more in the developing countries owing to the relatively higher salaries there, is a source of serious economic concern.

In an interesting paper on 'The production process in education' (in D. Adams (ed.) *Education and National Development*: London, Routledge and Kegan Paul, 1971), Professor John Vaizey of Brunel University, England, points out that economists, not least, have seen to it that the inputs into the educational systems are kept under control in terms of quantity. On the output side, however, most of the work is still to be done. 'The way in which the inputs are transmuted into outputs is largely an area of ignorance.' This is one of the main reasons why, particularly in the present stage of the IEA survey work, the main emphasis will be laid on attempts to disentangle what factors within the school system, such as teaching, material resources and staff availability, account for differences between schools as well as between students in terms of educational attainments. The overall aim is to identify the malleable factors, that is to say those factors that can be affected by policy decisions and which seem to play a prime role in bringing about differences between schools and even more so between students.

So far no comprehensive attempt has been made to measure the qualitative output of school education in developing countries and to relate such measures to strategic input factors, be they economic, social and/or pedagogical. Of particular interest in this connection are such factors (which together constitute school resources) as teacher competence, number of hours of instruction, class size, space available, teaching aids, etc. Before the end of 1974 we shall be in a position to provide precise information about the outcomes of the teaching of reading and science in some twenty countries, among them such countries as India, Iran, Chile and Thailand. Representative samples of children at the ages of ten, fourteen and eighteen have been given the same international tests, both cognitive and non-cognitive. It should be pointed out that the instruments have been carefully pretested in all the countries and that in each of them special national committees have dealt with the preparation of the instruments in co-operation with one international committee for each subject area included in the study. Precautions have been taken to remove test items which could be suspected of bias against a particular culture or country. Translation problems were given particular attention, not least when it came to the development of tests in reading comprehension. Incidentally, in an exploratory study it was found that, in so-called culture-free or culture-fair tests, between-country differences were more pronounced compared with within-country differences than they were in achievement tests in, for for instance, reading.

Recent surveys conducted both at the national and international level suggest that much more of the between-country and between-student variance than was previously assumed is attributable to conditions outside the influence of the school, such as the socioeconomic structure of the society outside the school, local per pupil expenditure, parental education and type of community – urban, rural or suburban. The Plowden Committee in England tried to account for the differences in achievement between 11 year old pupils and found that about two-thirds of the variance accounted for could be assigned to background factors of the type mentioned above, whereas only one-third could be assigned to what happened to the student at school. And, as is well known in the United States, similar findings were reported by Professor James S. Coleman and his associates. By and large the IEA mathematics survey confirmed the conclusions of the two national studies, as discussed by Dr Hendric Gïdeonse in an article in the *Teachers College Record* some years ago. The outcomes of the Coleman survey in particular gave rise to a fruitful methodological debate on the pitfalls and snags in multivariate analysis. The seemingly rather modest contributions of teaching per se to differences in student performance caused quite a lot of concern. A conference was organized under the auspices of the US Office of Education focusing on these problems. The proceedings were published under the title *Do Teachers Make a Difference?* (US Department of Health, Education and Welfare, US Government Printing Office, 1970).

On the basis of these and other surveys we can expect widely different levels of attainment between developed and less developed countries, simply because they differ tremendously in sociocultural structure and therefore in the socioeconomic background of students. The broad occupational sectors in developed countries are the manufacturing and service industries, whereas the developing countries are dominated by an agricultural subsistence economy. Even school resources and teacher competencies equivalent to those in Europe or the United States would by no means suffice to bring the children anywhere near the level of achievement of those from the more wealthy countries. In reading comprehension, for instance, 10 year olds in the developing countries with about the same amount of full-time schooling (in terms of school years) as their coevals in Europe and the US lag at least one standard deviation behind. This means, then, that the mean performance in some of the more advanced developing countries is equivalent to the fifteenth percentile of the distribution of reading scores in, for instance, most European countries. It should, once again, be emphasized that such a gap is to a large extent attributable to socioeconomic differences and should therefore not be surprising. The practical implication of this is that education cannot serve as a substitute for social and economic reform.

The present IEA survey is not an international horse race; rather, we are trying to take advantage of differences on the input side of a series of educational systems in order to account for differences on the output side. The interesting point, therefore, is how certain strategic input factors are related to output and how much of it they account for.

The high price paid for the products of formal schooling in developing countries in terms of high rates of drop-out and grade-repeating has in recent years inspired several attempts to try out alternative strategies which could take better advantage of the resources available and lead to outcomes more relevant to the social and economic needs of a given country. Importing reform models from the wealthy countries does not help very much, because such new strategies tend to be both skill-intensive and capital-intensive. The developing countries have a shortage of both these types of resources.

One has recently begun to question the very metaphysics of the European schooling approach. The interest that several international and national technical assistance agencies have begun to show in non-formal or out-of-school education is an important symptom. Programmes in, for instance, alphabetization, where the common denominator is a better integration of education and working life, have already been launched and more 'non-formal education' will probably follow.

Intelligence of another kind 5

We live in a society where more and more people will have
to educate themselves for continuously growing periods.
No wonder many are asking whether the supply of talent
will really meet the need. In our time most people still
essentially regard a person's talent as intellectual capital
transmitted by heredity. Hence, to quote a colleague of
mine from New Zealand, our educational institutions
cannot 'fight against nature'; in other words, they cannot
take youngsters beyond the highest rung of the
educational ladder that inherited talent has established.
Most educators look on talent as the ability to absorb
the knowledge communicated by the school.

Some have begun to wonder how things will go for the
'unintelligent', defined as those of low scholastic ability
who find it difficult to keep up when courses swell and
the statutory number of years in school increases. For the
economists, a big problem is how society should set about
getting enough educated and clever people to man the
rapidly expanding number of jobs of a professional kind.
On the assumption that present tendencies will continue,
we find for instance that in a country like Sweden more
than half the cohorts will soon be passing through the

university-preparing *gymnasium*, while one-third will then go on to the universities and professional schools. In another two decades or so it is likely that nearly one-quarter of all jobs will require university training.

It is not our intention here to explore the heredity–environment complex as it affects mental traits, far less to demonstrate all the social implications this question has. But it is still worth calling attention to some new facets illuminated by latter-day empirical research and theoretical approaches. The behavioural scientists were long split, and to a large extent still are, into two schools of thought based on heredity and environment respectively. For the most part the former were to be found in England and the latter in America – if they were psychologists. If sociology was their field, then they were and are preoccupied with environmental theory on both sides of the Atlantic. The British psychologist, Cyril Burt, taking studies of twins as his main base, has indefatigably sought to show that about 80 per cent of the variation in intellectual achievement is accounted for by inherited factors and the rest by environment. In the United States Harold Skeels has recently followed up foster children for more than twenty years to demonstrate that environment can work dramatic changes in intellectual performance as measured by so-called intelligence tests.

Talent and social class according to Jensen

The pendulum of American thinking has begun to swing away from the environmental school. A team of investigators under Arthur Jensen, a psychologist at the University of California, Berkeley, has been delving into the question of differences of intelligence between groups, for instance social classes and races. At the same time their observations of children from different socioeconomic groups have led them to revise their concept of intelligence itself. Jensen has made a comprehensive presentation of his case in the 1969 winter issue of the *Harvard Educational Review* under the title 'How much can we boost IQ and scholastic achievement?'.

Because of the way intelligence testing began, intelligence has traditionally been associated with achievement in school. The criterion of intelligent behaviour has been to do well in the classroom, and the validity of so-called intelligence tests has been determined by correlating the scores with school achievements. Test items which were poorly correlated with teacher ratings, marks or whatever else was used as criteria were regarded as unsuitable indices of intelligence compared with items which discriminated between good and bad pupils.

Jensen now raises a question loaded with political and emotional dynamite: do inherited differences of talent exist between certain groups (social classes, let us say) and, if so, to what extent? He puts the question for a specific reason: if a society confers greater opportunities on each of its members not only to obtain an education but also to carve out a social career according to his aptitudes, must we then not also assume that genetic differences will ultimately make themselves felt in the life career and in social mobility? He points to three circumstances which, though they do not answer his question affirmatively, could be embarrassing to those who want to answer it negatively.

First of all, only 30 per cent of individual differences in test scores — as shown by the standardization data published by Terman and Merrill — are accounted for by differences in socioeconomic background. In other words, 70 per cent of the individual differences lie *within* the social classes. If, as Burt purports to have shown with his twin-based data, 80 per cent of the differences are rooted in heredity, one can scarcely avoid discussing whether a considerable part of the differences between social classes may have a hereditary background.

Second, the incidence of what Francis Galton called the regression towards the mean suggests that differences of talent between socioeconomic groups may have an inheritable component. Considered as a genetic phenomenon, regression signifies that the children of parents who, for a given trait, belong to a group above or below the mean, tend to fall nearer the mean than their parents. For example, tall parents tend to have tall children, but the latter will cluster nearer the mean for their generation than their parents do – and conversely for parents of short stature. Proceeding from a polygenetic model such as Galton's, an investigator can predict that the regression for, say, intellectual achievement is bound to fall at half the distance between the parental mean and the population average. This prediction has proved to be correct for body-height data. In an essay written for the *British Journal of Statistical Psychology* in 1961, Burt professed to show that the model also holds for intelligence.

Third, Jensen points out that foster children who are tested after having spent many years in foster homes show IQs that correlate with ratings of the socioeconomic status of their biological parents. This correlation is no lower than for children raised by their biological parents.

A critique of Jensen's theses

A brief examination of Jensen's theses is now in order, the more so if one happens, like myself, to be aligned with the environmental school – where, incidentally, educators ought to find the climate more congenial for natural reasons. Against every one of Jensen's arguments, weighty objections can be raised. The present author has dealt with the heredity-environment issue more in detail in *Social Background and Educational Career* (Paris, OECD, 1972).

Let us begin with the argument that genetic factors determine the differences between socioeconomic groups and that 70–80 per cent of individual differences are inherited – as concluded from research into twins. If that is correct, the hereditary factors would account for more of the variation in school achievement than all the environmental factors together, including the factors that impinge on the pupil in the classroom. According to Dobzhansky, himself a geneticist, studies of twins underestimate the variation produced by the environment because identical twins, when brought up in different homes, usually end up in the same cultural pattern and often in the same social class. This means that there is from the outset a correlation within the pairs with regard to environmental factors. This is therefore added to the intra-pair correlation with regard to heredity. The correlations obtained within the pairs in a group of twins hold solely for this group and cannot be generalized for other populations. If we investigate a population that is rather homogeneous socially, the hereditary variation will come through more strongly than in a socially and culturally more heterogeneous population.

Jensen has made the mistake of regarding social class classification as an exhaustive measure of environmental variation. The different socioeconomic groups are tacitly considered homogeneous in environmental terms. That of course is not the case. Each of these groups subsumes immense variations of parental ambition, cultural stimuli and so on. Richard Wolf, who some years ago created a minor sensation with his study of children from different homes in the Chicago area, has shown that the inclusion of psychological variables makes it possible to attain correlations approaching +0·80 between home environment and school achievement; in other words, more than half the variance in school achievements can be explained by home environment.

The second argument, that on regression, seems at first glance to strike harder. Children of better-off parents move towards lower IQs on the average than children of the worse-off. But here the comparison is between generations who in many respects stem from widely diverse social backgrounds. There has occurred, in those countries which are relevant here, a levelling out of social conditions, and even more so of cultural ones. It follows that by and large the groups have been moving closer together. Indeed, it is doubtful whether any common reference point can be established between different generations where IQs are concerned.

The third argument, which has to do with the similarity between foster children and their biological parents notwithstanding the almost total absence of contact, also looks convincing, especially when the same correlation is said to hold for children who have been brought up by their biological parents. Apart from the fact that the correlation does not much exceed al ow +0·20 and therefore explains only about 4–5 per cent of the differences between individuals, the socioeconomic group makes a poor measure of environment – *nota bene* if one wants to study how much of the individual variation this explains. Furthermore, the same seems to hold for foster children as for adopted pair individuals of identical twins, namely that the two sets of homes tend to be correlated.

As Wolf and others have shown, the more environment that can be 'uncovered', the greater that part of the variation that can be explained by environment. I once made bold to remark in a book of mine, *Ability and Environment* (Stockholm, 1948), that, after the effects of environment have been identified the remnants of ignorance could be ascribed to 'heredity'. After the lapse of twenty-five years I am disposed to defend this thesis even more stoutly.

Learning ability and intelligence quotients

In 1966 Harold Skeels published the report of a follow-up of foster children whose acquaintance he first made at an orphanage in the early 1930s. All these children had been born out of wedlock to mothers from the bottom social stratum. After a period of two years, those who had been placed in good foster homes were found to have improved their IQs by an average 25 points, while those who stayed on in the orphanage had deteriorated appreciably. Skeels formed an experimental group of thirteen children from the good foster homes and a control group of twelve remaining at the orphanage, and followed their progress for twenty-one years. Social adjustment developed normally for all children in the experimental group. As adults their average IQ was 104. Nine of those in the control group were still in institutions.

If intelligence is supposed to be essentially conditioned by heredity, how can changes as dramatic as these be explained? According to Jensen, environment is to be regarded as a 'threshold variable'. Just as a certain minimum of calories and vitamins is needed for the normal physical development of a child, so does inherited ability need a minimum of certain psychological stimuli in the environment if it is to develop at all.

The study of group differences relating to intellectual performance has turned up wide variations between different types of test items. Thus big differences have been found between white and black schoolchildren in the US for their scores on verbal tests, whereas the differences on rote learning tests are small or non-existent. Jensen and his associates discovered a high correlation between conventional IQ and learning ability for children from advantageous environments, but a low or non-existent correlation for children from low socioeconomic groups. To put this finding in different terms, it means that children with low IQs from a high socioeconomic group are less able to learn than children from a low socioeconomic group, whereas the intergroup differences are small or non-existent among children who have high IQs (see the diagram).

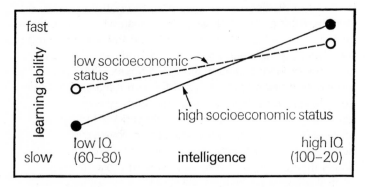

Illustrated above are the results arrived at by Jensen and his associates from their studies of group differences of learning ability. IQ and learning ability were found to correlate highly for children from favoured environments, but the correlation was low for children from environments of low socioeconomic status.

How shall this interesting phenomenon be explained? In a paper read before the 1967 convention of the American Educational Research Association on 'New approaches to the measurement of intelligence', Jensen presented a new theoretical model of intellectual performance as it functions in the educational context.

He distinguishes between 'fundamental learning ability', 'intelligence', 'docility' and 'educability'. Fundamental learning ability mainly refers to rote learning performance that is measured with ordinary experimental tests. However, this 'rote' learning cannot be directly converted into 'educability', i.e., translated into school achievements, but must first be channelled through 'intelligence' and

'docility'. 'Intelligence' is to be partly regarded as a group
of acquired skills, which all boil down to rational 'data-
processing' of the information received. Stimulation from
the near environment — for instance that given by parents
when they talk often to the child, systematically broaden
his range of experience and try to develop his linguistic
skill — gives the child the instruments he needs to
comprehend the environment and adapt himself to it.
Given the 'learning set' shaped by the home, the school
can go on from there with the conceptual and abstract
learning that goes into, or should go into, most of the
knowledge it communicates. But in addition there is a
need for the skills that constitute what Jensen calls
'trainability', and what I have preferred to call 'docility':
the pupil's ability to control attention conditionally, to
train himself to repeat what he is learning and so on.

These are the skills that mainly set off the culturally
unfavoured and meagerly stimulated children from those
who grow up under favoured circumstances. On the other
hand, the two categories are not far apart where 'rote'
learning ability is concerned.

In commenting on Jensen's research Carl Bereiter has
pointed out that due consideration of the existence of two
levels of learning can have far-reaching implications for
classroom learning. Too much teaching draws upon
verbal-abstract ability, constituted by cognitive factors
measured by IQ tests, when effective learning could easier
be achieved by simple memorization. In a way, the
former approach discriminates against those who profit
more from the latter.

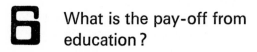

6   What is the pay-off from education?

Education and income

Some years ago American newspapers published a report from an economic conference in Washington, DC. One of the participants had tried to calculate the 'life income' that a university degree could be expected to yield by comparison with a high school diploma. The average return on investment in such an education was estimated at $120,000. The lecturer also purported to prove that the money spent on four years of higher education produced a higher pay-off than if it were invested in shares.

The rationale behind these figures is far from being a new phenomenon in the United States. Ever since the economists began to interest themselves in education as a 'self-investment' or as 'human capital formation', the value of higher education for both the individual and the community at large has been preached with mounting fervour.

That education can account for half the rate of economic growth has been music to the ears of those who contend — no doubt rightly — that it deserves more accelerated investment as compared with other public sectors. According to their argument, both society and the individual stand to gain if relatively more of the income from tax goes on education.

However, the question of how education pays off for the individual can also be seen as a problem of 'fair shares'. If, as is true of us in Sweden, we regard education at all stages as a public service provided free of charge, and one that is augmented into the bargain by a system of subsidies which partially indemnifies for the income lost by staying longer in school, is it then equitable that the better educated should receive much higher pay? After all, they have in most cases financed their own studies to a slight extent only, in some cases not at all. This matter came up a few years ago in a debate on meritocracy which appeared in the Swedish periodical, *Studiekamraten*. One of the contributors, Dr Per Holmberg of the Swedish Confederation of Trade Unions, cited figures from the 1960 census. Gainfully employed men in the age group from forty to fifty earned an average 16,400 kronor per year irrespective of education, while those who held a higher academic degree came up to 53,600 kronor. An income gap this wide prompted the rhetorical question: can it be fair and reasonable to pay the PhD several times as much as the working man?

Given the values to which all people profess allegiance, if only with their lips, the answer is also given: no, it is not fair and reasonable – *provided the differences of income stem solely or mainly from differences of education.* The underlined *caveat* is important since many consider it self-evident that differences of income between groups with varying educational attainments are *solely* attributable to these attainments. In the following pages I shall demonstrate that this assumption, made under the social conditions that have prevailed up to now – and they, of course, are implicitly embodied by the figures cited above – is highly dubious.

If someone should come up with the idea of finding out

what people who belong to, say, the Rotary or the Royal Automobile Club earn in average income, he would scarcely be surprised to learn that their members rank higher on the income scale than the rest of the community. I assume no one would make the absurd contention that membership of these organizations explains the higher incomes. But that is precisely what many people, including even some economists, argue in substance when they venture to explain why people of higher education also have higher pay or income generally. This logical error crops up quite often in social science research, and is even more common in politically charged discussions of social phenomena. A British colleague with a vested interest in Latin once called my attention to the many eminent politicians and businessmen in his country who had taken their degrees in classical languages at Oxford or Cambridge. I was tactless enough to tell him that they might well have achieved eminence *in spite of* having studied classical languages. They could also have reached the top for other reasons.

Similar objections may be raised against those who argue as though formal education were the only income-differentiating factor. It is reasonable to assume that a series of other factors also, among them family background, intellectual ability and level of aspiration, essentially determine differences not only of income, but also of life career in general. In analysing the pay-off from education, American economists have found that blacks tend to constitute an exception to the rule that much higher incomes go to those with a university education than to those without it. The usual explanation for this disparity is that blacks are discriminated against on the labour market and do not receive pay in line with their qualifications. But a closer look at the research data reveals that the higher-educated blacks tend to come from a lower socioeconomic group than whites in the same category. The difference of income between whites and blacks of similar educational attainment would therefore appear to be chiefly due to social background.

From ten to thirty-six: a sociological study

In Sweden a cohort of 1,500 people has been regularly followed up (for thirty-six years at the time of writing) to explain the significance of home background, intelligence and schooling for variations of income earned at the age of thirty-five. (T. Husén *et al., Talent, Opportunity, and Career:* Stockholm, Almqvist & Wiksell, 1969.) Their social background, test scores and school records were surveyed when they attended grade 3 in Malmö in 1938, at which time their average age was ten. Their progress up through the grades and later on in life has been under study ever since. The overriding aim of this project is to find out whether conditions going as far back as the age of ten, such as parental background and IQ, can predict the further course of education and career, and if so to what extent. We had access to information on the incomes of these persons when they were 36 years old. Considering the variations that arise from year to year, it would have been in order to employ an average, say, of income earned over five years. But as we shall see presently, the available yardstick still provides us with not a little useful information. In processing the data we separated the income-earners by sex because many of the women have part-time jobs. Although the findings we present are restricted to men, it turns out that the role played by education does not differ as between the two sexes. As indicated above, a complete report of the study has been published. We therefore confine ourselves below to the more important tabulations.

The income-earners were divided into four classes by full-time education: less than eight years, eight to ten, eleven to fourteen and more than fourteen years. Average incomes for the four classes were:

less than 8 years	15,800 kronor
8–10 years	18,600 kronor
11–14 years	25,200 kronor
more than 14 years	40,400 kronor

This is a familiar picture. The much higher income level in our fourth class, of course, is identified with those who have gone on to university or professional school. Smaller differences of income obtain between those who completed secondary school and elementary school respectively.

Next, we classify the subjects by socioeconomic group. Group 1 comprises professionals, executives and proprietors of big enterprises. Group 2 comprises white collar workers. Group 3 comprises manual workers with skilled jobs, and group 4 those with unskilled manual jobs. This gives us the following series of means:

socioeconomic group 1	34,600 kronor
socioeconomic group 2	18,400 kronor
socioeconomic group 3	17,500 kronor
socioeconomic group 4	15,300 kronor

Although the spread here is lower than the one observed for educational levels, the difference between group 1 and the other three is quite substantial. To all appearances, a person who wants to make money not only needs a good education but also has to choose the right parents! If we cross-tabulate social background with education, we can pinpoint the intergroup variation of income which exists at each educational level. It turns out that most of those with a higher education come from socioeconomic group 1. Their income averages about 50 per cent higher than that earned by members of the three other groups with the same education. Among those who went to school for eleven to fourteen years, those with a parental background in socioeconomic group 1 averaged twice the income earned by members of group 4.

Thus income level would appear to correlate just as strongly with social background as with education. But what about intellectual (or scholastic) ability, which in this case was measured by a simple test at the age of ten? On the basis of the intelligence quotients we made a classification on a five-point scale: high ability, above average ability, average ability, below average ability and ow ability. Our first observation was that those with high IQs when they were ten tended to earn higher incomes when they were thirty-five. The differences were not particularly small. Among those who completed secondary education, members of the highest IQ group were earning incomes more than 50 per cent higher than in the lowest group. On the whole, intelligence seems to differentiate incomes more at the higher educational levels than at the lower. When we cross-tabulate socioeconomic group with intelligence quotient, we find that tested ability at ten is associated with adult income level within the socioeconomic groups. Hence the income differences between ability levels are not solely explainable by differences of socioeconomic background and formal education. Conclusion: the type of ability measured by so-called intelligence tests administered early, with due account taken of school level and social background, helps to explain differences of income at the age of thirty-five.

By now I trust I have adduced evidence sufficient, if nothing else, to cast doubt on the notion of the all-determining effects of education. Unfortunately we have no data on parental attitudes to education and their social aspirations in 1938. In 1964 we asked members of our studied population, who were then 36 years old, about how much education they wanted for *their* children. The disclosed level of aspiration was consistently high, a fact that reflects the changing attitudes to education among members of lower socioeconomic groups in Sweden during the past years. Yet we find a remarkable correlation between what this second generation hoped for from its children and its own social background. The number in each socioeconomic group who wanted a higher education for their children were:

Socioeconomic group			
1	2	3	4
78%	46%	36%	32%

Note the very high level of aspiration in group 1 (upper and upper middle class) compared with 3 and 4 (semiskilled and skilled workers).

One of the arguments advanced in Sweden in the debate about meritocracy is that instruments of wage policy ought to be engaged to reduce the income gap between educational groups. Far be it from me to render a final opinion on a problem as intricate as this. But if variations in formal education only partially explain differences in pay and income, any measures to level them out amount in effect to a kind of penalty tax on ability and ambition.

Lastly, it might be in order to say a few words about the relation between education and social mobility that we can expect in the future. The subjects of our longitudinal study have seen their lives bear heavy imprints of their social origin, for all the social mobility that has taken place. Most of those who were born in socioeconomic group 1 qualified for university entrance, while only the exceptional member of group 3 or 4 went as far as attending a *gymnasium* (upper secondary school). But what is going to happen to the children born of our follow-ups? The overwhelming majority in all socioeconomic groups will stay in school until the end of their teens. A reasonable assumption is that intellectual ability and talent

for keeping up both in education and work will mean more
for them in relative terms than family background. Should
we venture to study the social status achieved at the age
of thirty-five by the children of our third graders in the
mid-1990s, we should presumably find a higher correlation
with intellectual ability than was observed for their
parents.

The internationalization of education

The internationalization of education

Before World War II, schooling and education were
provincial and national concerns to an eminent degree;
in some countries, indeed, they were regarded as matters
that only local authorities and agencies need trouble
themselves with. With the inception of aid programmes for
the developing countries, of the international organizations
such as UNESCO, FAO, the OECD and the Council of
Europe, and – not least – of enormously expanded
communications through the mass media and foreign
travel, educational problems have come to be more
international. In the mid-1960s the United States and
Europe were playing host to about 250,000 university
students from other parts of the world. As school politicians
and educators have become aware of the bearing that
education has on social and economic progress, they are
increasingly concerned to cross national frontiers to
exchange experiences and to learn from one another. It is
a revealing commentary that comparative education, the
field of study which compares educational systems in
different countries so as to arrive at generalized conclusions
on how these systems are functioning and developing, did
not really amount to much until after 1945. As for

educational planning, which is that segment of national public planning concerned with the allocation of resources to schools and other seats of learning, as well as their organization and course content, it did not get off the ground until after 1950. The International Institute for Educational Planning, a body supported by UNESCO, the Ford Foundation and the World Bank, was established as recently as 1962.

I shall not in this connection examine latter-day educational developments in the modern industrial or advanced countries (the A-countries) or in the developing countries (D-countries). I shall confine myself to looking into the altered determinants of education that have made themselves so strongly felt in the A-countries, but that have also come to have repercussions in the D-countries, especially through the medium of assistance programmes sponsored by the A-countries.

Education in today's world

Up to the middle of this century education was largely regarded as 'consumption'. Higher education was considered a prerogative of the higher social classes. It constituted an integral part of the very status they held, not a condition for attaining that status. Once one of the driving forces of mercantilism was a tendency to regard educated ability as an investment that could help promote the growth of national manufactures. Economists did not, however, begin to study the role of education in economic growth until much later. The classical school of economic thought sought to explain this growth in terms of two essential factors : the availability of capital and the availability of labour, but with no allowance made for the latter's quality. More recently, however, economists such as Theodore Schultz in the United States, Friedrich Edding in Germany and Ingvar Svennilson in Sweden have applied somewhat different methods in order to demonstrate that education accounted for a very big share of economic growth, perhaps more than 50 per cent when research was added.

In the years since 1945 education has come to be regarded by the A-countries as a dynamic factor of the first rank, and rightly so. Before long the second industrial revolution, with electronics and cybernetics as its mainsprings, will have done away with practically all unskilled work and generated an enormously increased demand for skilled manpower. During the 1930s, a decade of stagnating and inflationary economics, the skilled and unskilled ran equal risks of losing their jobs. Today things are the other way round. People with a poor background of general education are incapable of assimilating the advanced vocational training that everybody needs and, still worse, they are unable to be retrained. On the university and college level we now have a phenomenon that can only be described as mass education. In the past two decades or so, most of the A-countries have known only too well what the 'educational explosion' means. Enrolments in secondary schools and universities have skyrocketed. In the United States, where only 7 per cent of every cohort graduated from high school around the turn of the century, about 75 per cent now attend school up to the age of eighteen. In Sweden the population of university students has increased from 20,000 in 1956 to 110,000 in 1969.

Obviously, the mushrooming demand for education is conditioned not only by its greater 'market value', which is a way of saying that people in A-countries now find it easier to get higher-grade jobs, and also to be retrained for another occupation if their own should disappear or take on a radically different guise in consequence of structural changes in the economy; but also, to an essential degree, education remains consumption: the endeavour to broaden

one's horizons and to improve one's general orientation.
This is particularly striking in the affluent countries, where
the majority of teenagers go to school. It also partly
explains why educational costs per pupil have increased.

The knowledge explosion

Scientific research has likewise grown with explosive force
since 1940. A widely quoted statement says that more than
90 per cent of the scientists who have been active since
the birth of Christ are still alive. Reference is often made to
a 'knowledge explosion'. As measured by the number of
scientific reports and publications, the 'split period' for the
accumulation of learning in many disciplines is less than
ten years, i.e., the corpus of knowledge doubles every
tenth year. At the same time many disciplines are
ramifying into increasingly specialized segments. To give an
example, the liberal arts faculties of Swedish universities in
1907 awarded degrees in some twenty subjects. By the
mid-1960s the number of subjects had exceeded 100. Since
the early 1950s the resources allotted to research in most
A-countries have doubled at the rate of once every five years.

Naturally, it must not be assumed that the corpus of
knowledge which comprises 'learning' in any one subject
is being enlarged with new increments only. Much of the
pre-existing subject matter must necessarily be revised in
the light of rapid scientific advances. This is bound to have
certain consequences for schools and universities. As late
as a century ago it was still possible to maintain an
encyclopedic cultural and learning ideal, with its
implications of a 'liberal education' that was supposed to
impart familiarity with all areas of learning, or at least
mastery of their 'fundamental facts'. But with the swelling
of subject matter there came the problem not only of
screening out irrelevant topics, but also of imparting it in a
different way from before. The matter at issue nowadays
turns less on teaching the pupils 'facts' in the encyclopedic

sense than on teaching them the fundamental concepts, principles and theoretical 'models' which inform a given area of learning, to teach that area as a discipline. To a greater extent, too, it becomes a question of teaching the pupils to seek knowledge by themselves and of how to fit that knowledge into what they have already learned. This signifies a shift from learning specific cognitive data to learning the skills which are bound up with the acquisition of knowledge itself. An overriding task of our schools of today is to impart to the students the skill of learning how to acquire learning.

Up to our time the years of childhood and youth were thought to be the period of exclusive preparation for adult life — a preparation consisting of going to school and training for a future occupation. The things that were learned then were supposed to function as intellectual nourishment for the rest of life's journey. Correspondingly, in the years of adulthood it was too late to learn anything. But a conspicuous feature of today's changing society is the rapid transformation of economic life — and indeed of our daily living habits — being wrought by science and technology. For instance, unskilled jobs in assembly-line production as well as in the service sector are disappearing as machines take over more and more of the operations involved. Cybernetics and computer technology provide a framework for skilful flexibility and creative work in areas where previously tedious routines predominated. New occupations are emerging and others are fading away in consequence of the technological changes and/or the changes in consumption that will follow from them. Many of the occupations or jobs in which young people will be engaged as adults simply do not exist, and can hardly be foreseen, when they go to school. Constant provision for further training must be made even in the enduring occupations, so that their practitioners will be able to keep up with the latest developments. As a result, continuing education generally, and vocational education in particular, has become increasingly common in adult life.

Be that as it may, an important part of adult education retains a more mind-broadening objective. That accounts for the very large scope of independent and optional programmes of adult education in evening classes, study circles and lecture courses. Robert Hutchins has defined education as an activity whereby human beings learn to become more intelligent. It is quite legitimate to say that life in the society of the economically developed countries has come to be one long continuation school. In the United States, where a survey of adult education was undertaken at the University of Chicago in the early 1960s, it was found that more than one out of every five adults had taken part in organized studies after leaving regular school. Most of the enrolments were in part-time courses given after working hours. The subjects studied were equally divided between the bread-and-butter type on the one hand and the generally broadening and recreational on the other.

The democratization of educational opportunities

Education over and above the compulsory is no longer the prerogative of an élite, whether it be a social, economic or cultural one. To the extent that opportunities have been opened up it has become more democratic. This in effect means that governments have sought to remove more of the economic and other material obstacles that have prevented young people of disadvantaged backgrounds from continuing their education beyond compulsory schooling. Thus many countries have abolished tuition fees at all levels. However, the will and ability to acquire a higher education depends not only on the financial resources at a student's command, but also on the attitudes to such education, not least those of his parents. It is common knowledge that the better-off sections of the community are greatly overrepresented in the higher education of countries where 'equal opportunity' formally exists. There are two reasons for this: first, young people of poorer means do not stem from the same educationally conscious environment, and hence compete less frequently for the often limited admissions to universities and professional schools; and second, it is actually more difficult for them to hold their own in this competition owing to the less favourable cultural influences that the home has exercised on their previous scholastic achievements. According to the Plowden Report, which presented the findings of an exhaustive inquiry into the British junior school, covering the age range from five to eleven, at least half the differences in scholastic achievement at the age of eleven are accounted for by the social background of pupils in general and the educational ambitions of parents in particular. Hence the school can do no more than function as a limited 'corrective' of the profound influences exerted in the home. It cannot serve as a substitute for social reform.

Education in the economically advanced countries has come to be an instrument for social climbing. The school of a former day was an adjunct of ascriptive status, i.e. it constituted a natural part of the social status to which one was born, so to speak. But now that education is supposed to promote upward social mobility, there has been increasing discussion in many countries of the so-called meritocracy problem. To an ever growing extent, power and influence tend to accrue to the educated experts. More and more of the job openings in today's society are reserved for people of high educational qualifications.

New teaching technology

Over the course of time the conditions which govern teaching have not proved immune to the 'technological explosion'. The very inculcation of knowledge has been affected by the advent of new media such as radio and television. Individualized approaches to classroom work have been facilitated by the use of new devices such as tape recorders, teaching machines and different kinds of projectors, permitting the student to set his own pace and choose his own media for developing proficiency in languages, mathematics and other subjects. Efforts to create a new teaching technology are making more and more headway. This not only means that the various aids have been integrated into the teaching process, but that the process itself is being carefully analysed with reference to objectives, selection of subject matter, didactic methods and evaluation. The force of all these innovations has been metamorphosing the teacher's role. He tends less to act as the direct mediator or transmitter of knowledge and more as the 'creator of learning opportunities', that is, as the person who plans, guides and evaluates the acquisition of knowledge by his pupils. That in turn puts greater emphasis on the self-activity and independent learning of students. It is now increasingly appreciated that teaching and learning are by no means identical.

The work of international organizations

Since the end of World War II a number of international organizations have variously fostered interchange across borders in the educational sphere. These interchanges have not been concerned solely with experiences and know-how but also with the organization of assistance to the developing countries. UNESCO, the UN agency for cultural, scientific and educational matters, has played an important role in both these respects. This organization has also published a *World Survey of Education*, which gives detailed data on the school organization, educational facilities etc. of member countries. In addition, UNESCO has undertaken various initiatives for the improvement of curricula, teacher training and so on. It has also been active in exploring the potential and feasibility of technical assistance to developing countries in the educational field. UNESCO has sponsored several major conferences to consider steps to eliminate illiteracy in Africa and Asia. Working in close collaboration with UNESCO are the UNESCO Institute for Education in Hamburg and the International Institute for Educational Planning in Paris. The former organizes international conferences on important educational issues, and was instrumental in the genesis of studies that have been carried out by the International Association for the Evaluation of Educational Achievement (IEA). This project first bore fruit in 1967, when the findings of a twelve-nation empirical study on the teaching of mathematics were published. Here the achievements of pupils were related not only to pedagogical factors such as course content, teacher qualifications and classroom schedules, but also to social and economic factors in the respective countries. The Organization for Economic Co-operation and Development (OECD), which embraces most of Western Europe as well as the United States and Japan, has performed seminal work in illuminating the significance of education for economic growth. The OECD has also initiated research into the utilization of talents in different countries and the mutual exchange of experiences in the educational sphere. A salient feature of this work is its use of 'country examiners', whose members function as critical examiners of the educational system in a country that is not their own. Lastly, it can be mentioned that the Council of Europe Secretariat in Strasbourg has a department of culture and education. The council also organizes conferences where the member country ministers of education meet regularly.

2 Education in developing countries

The current picture

Ivan Illich, former president of the Catholic University of
Puerto Rico and a member of a research team which
was studying Latin American problems, wrote an article on
education published by the *Saturday Review* in early 1968.
Its very title was provocative: 'The futility of schooling in
Latin America'. Illich propounds two main theses as
follows: first, investment in the school systems of Latin
America, which in some of its countries absorbs more
than one-third of current government expenditure and
which has high priority in foreign assistance programmes
(by the World Bank, for example), is misdirected. It does
not restructure the economy and level out social differences
as is intended. It favours an admittedly growing yet still
small middle class and serves to alienate the large and
rapidly growing masses who can no longer make their
living from agriculture. The masses are drawn instead to the
cities, where they cannot be absorbed by manufacturing
industry and become at best a service proletariat. The
drop-out rate is high in most schools. To an ever increasing
extent, the schools represent a grading, screening and

élite-promoting meritocracy in the same way that used to obtain in France, when the third estate broke through the feudal barrier and in its turn began to raise barriers against other classes. In consequence the Latin American school tends to widen rather than narrow the gaps between different sections of the community. In other words, only a small minority reaps the full benefits of all the investment made in education, which political propaganda likes to portray as of extreme importance for all citizens. Any leader who calls for restraint or for a different pattern of investment risks committing political suicide.

On the same day I wrote down my comments on Illich's article I received a letter from a young scholar, who for some time had been trying to set up an agency for educational planning and related research in a Latin American country under the US AID (Agency for International Development). His use of the word 'technicians' refers to the social science experts who served on the team with him. He wrote:

> Given the present division of labour, with politicians working in the Ministry of Education and technicians in the Institute of Planning, educational planning is pushed aside. The politicians have a near total investment in the *status quo*, while the technicians are looking for 'catharsis' as they develop utopian and comprehensive plans to have education transform a society that will continue to sail under the flags of the conquistadors with exploitation and class privileges.

Second – and this is Illich's cardinal thesis – it may well be asked whether *schools* in the conventional sense are mainly needed to attain the aims of increased democracy and a restructured economy. 'It is difficult to tackle the school as a system', Illich writes, 'because we are so accustomed to it.' What he casts doubt on is the school in its present form: a building where children devote years full-time from morning to afternoon taking lessons and being examined by teachers. That is much too costly a form of education for developing countries, he holds, especially if it is to be suddenly given – on paper – to everyone within the framework of a scarce economy. Further, considering the social background of the pupils, conventional school education is much too ineffective. Last but not least, considering what the pupils will be doing in the future much of the education is irrelevant. Latin America, and Africa too, abound in examples of how large parts of the cohorts have not been schooled for occupations that may become meaningful in the foreseeable future. The general education given in many developing countries has no relevance for an economy that will remain agrarian for a long time to come, and where education should accordingly be made to help improve agriculture.

Then why are they all so eager to implement universal schooling at all costs in the developing countries, and not only at primary but also at secondary level? According to Illich, they are misled by what he calls the liberal myth. This has purportedly translated itself into reality in certain industrial countries (first and foremost the United States), in that education in these places leads to social advancement and equality at the same time as it helps to improve both the individual and society.

Alternatives to the traditional school

If not schools, then what? After all, we cannot readily extirpate a system embracing institutions called schools in which pupils receive full-time instruction from persons called teachers, who are trained for this purpose. Nor does Illich come up with any very revolutionary ideas on this score. But as he sees it there is a strong need for sweeping reforms that allow for the special social conditions in developing countries. He proposes two kinds of reform. One calls for the participation of industry and business, to a quite different extent from in the past, in the providing of a useful education. This involves not only giving work experience of the kind upper grade secondary school pupils receive in some advanced countries as part of their practical vocational guidance, but also calling in industry to impart the vocational skills that are directly useful. The resulting gain would be the greater number of young people taking education that prepares them for duties in the job world. For that purpose financial grants would be payable to firms, which would have to submit to controls to ensure that they keep up their end of the bargain. In addition there would be teaching-learning co-operation between the government and business communities.

The second proposal calls for measures to give more adults a fundamental education. Experiences of work with such education in the developing countries are indeed encouraging. Because adults more strongly sense the relevance of what they learn compared with the younger generation, they are as a rule more highly motivated. They are also able to put subject matter into the context of problems they face in life's harsher school. Finally: experiences of literacy programmes indicate that adults with adequate motivation learn more quickly than children.

Apart from these arguments Illich gives no background for his proposal to let industry take over an essential part of the schooling in developing countries. Many of the experts engaged in technical assistance programmes are so ethnocentric as to find inconceivable any form of schooling other than the one they have in their highly industrialized and economically advanced homelands. The experts forget that the developed parts of Europe introduced compulsory schooling only about a century or so ago, that it covered a fairly small portion of the calendar year, and that it ran for only a few years. The compulsory school was a place exclusively dedicated to implanting certain basic skills, such as reading, writing and arithmetic, as well as a grasp of specified subject matter, especially in Christianity. Upbringing and schooling were otherwise left to the family. It was there that the vast majority of young people also learned what they needed to cope with adult responsibilities – apart from the cases where they were indentured as apprentices to a master craftsman. Considering that the economies of developing countries are still dominated by agriculture and will be so for a long time to come, and that most of the non-farm employment will be provided by small workshops rather than factories, the creation of an institutionalized school system based on advanced-country models is a highly unrealistic enterprise. In the industrialized and urbanized society the family's educative functions are already diminished by the fact that the father, and to a growing extent the mother too, work outside the home. But that has not yet happened in the developing countries, which means that the home and the closely knit family group can contribute more to education than their counterparts in the industrial society. But even in such a society the system can be more widely used, as demonstrated not least by experiences from the Soviet Union.

I would not have discoursed on Illich at this length were it not that his train of thought largely parallels the one I have sought to develop, and which to my mind also has partial application to the advanced countries. In an era characterized by the second industrial revolution and the educational explosion, these countries are wrestling with problems that resemble those of the developing world but on a magnified scale. It is not only that more and more young people are taking a longer full-time education. The years devoted to education are also turning out more and more expensive. In consequence education has come to impose increasingly greater strains on real economic and financial resources. That has necessitated not only rumination but also some action relating to the more economical use of the resources available. We must thereby aim to carry out what I usually call a 'dynamic rationalization', which means trying to get more value for money spent even if the absolute costs per pupil and year go up. The need is for rationalization – in other words more efficient use of given resources – that will obviate drastic cuts in the quality of the products turned out by the educational system.

For that reason the first task for a 'profit improvement' programme should be to streamline teacher-led instruction, since that is the biggest item of expenditure. How should one go about reducing classroom time, especially at the teenage stage, without lowering the quality of skills and knowledge assimilated by the pupils? The gist of various reform proposals I have elaborated is to bring young people into earlier touch with adult activities, to enable them to enter into what I call 'functional participation'. Further, efforts must be made to get away from the ingrown notion that all education must be imparted before the age of twenty. Many youngsters can wait until adulthood, when a great deal can be perceived and learnt with greater relevance. Lastly, we must draw upon the reinforcing role played by the mass media, which can be given many more educational tasks to perform.

3 Meritocracy in the learning society: the USSR, the USA and Sweden

I don't know whether the term 'meritocracy' was first coined by the British sociologist, Michael Young. If not, it certainly made an impact as a catchword in his book *The Rise of the Meritocracy*. It is a book that is at once amusing and disquieting. Its style is that of the earnest and seemingly uncommitted social scientist, solemn even when the absurdities of unimaginative bureaucracy are being thoroughly detailed. This approach is all the more effective since the book is meant to be a pungent satire on a society where careers are crucially determined by ability and education, after birth and wealth have been put out of the running. Although the book should be read mainly as an exercise in polemics, it is capable of interpretation on several levels. I have met centrally placed bureaucrats whose day-to-day work is to plan for the educational system, who have been annoyed because they don't know whether Young is 'serious' or not. He no doubt is serious, in the sense that he has wanted to show what can happen if ability and education are unimaginatively and bureaucratically permitted to decide careers and social status. Nor has he been averse to the idea that our present efforts to exploit ability resources, and to give one and all

as much education as they can stand, will inevitably lead
to a meritocratic system.

Young describes how ever increasing sophistication is
being applied towards replacing seniority, age and general
background with current measurable ability in the hiring
and promotion of employees. The fundamental principle
for the whole system is that all people must have equal
opportunities to school themselves. Those who stay on in
school are given government subsidies which are
competitive with wages from work. Special pains are taken
to screen out the really topflight talents for enrolment in
the public schools that were formerly reserved for the
hereditary aristocracy and well-heeled upper class. Within
this top stratum, particular solicitude is shown for the
scientists and technologists thrown up by a kind of
Chinese machinery of intelligence ratings, qualifications and
examinations.

At the bottom of this new status pyramid a new
proletariat emerges : the untalented and unschooled. In
the society of an earlier day, the unskilled assembly-line
worker could console himself with the thought that a
better job was not his because he did not have the
opportunity to obtain the necessary basic education. The
meritocratic society does not even give him that hook on
which to hang his self-esteem. He *has* been given the
opportunity. If he hasn't taken advantage of it, the
responsibility, and blame, are his own. But when by the
year 2000 society has become so highly rationalized and
machine-controlled that there are no jobs left for those
with IQs below the average, the idea will be to make
these unskilled individuals useful by giving them tasks
that the skilled should not have to waste their time on,
such as charring, washing dishes and shining
shoes . . .

In Sweden, public measures to promote universal
schooling have given cause for alarm in certain quarters

lest they overemphasize the academic side and thereby pave the way for meritocracy. Among politicians and planners, the spectre of meritocracy is a projection of their alarm at the unexpected educational explosion and the overwhelming claims on resources it has brought in its train.

It may be appropriate at this juncture to reflect on the question, are we or are we not headed towards a meritocracy? Here the term is understood to mean that, in relative terms, education and ability confer greater influence, power and money – in short, social status – than social background, birth and inherited wealth. I think it was a sociologist who a few years ago said that education and ability have become the democratic substitutes for birth and wealth in our present-day society. The thesis I shall seek to elaborate below is that, given the definition just cited, we are inexorably moving towards a meritocracy. After touching on the factors which govern education in the modern, highly technological society, I shall briefly consider conditions in the Soviet Union, the United States and Sweden.

The modern society and education

A distinctive feature of present-day society is its increasing technicalization. Tasks of a routine nature are becoming fewer, while the tasks that are left require better qualifications of the people who perform them. Access to education has more and more become equal to all, at least formally, and that in turn has contributed to increased social mobility. The greater the equality of opportunity provided to get ahead regardless of social origin, and the more it becomes in the public interest to nurture talents, the better these talents will be turned to account in all social strata.

The modern society is also distinguished by a high degree

of change and mobility. Most striking is the occupational mobility that follows in the wake of increased economic rationalization and advanced technology. Further education and retraining are becoming more and more common. In the modern society, too, individual horizons of experience are immensely broadened by the mass media. To a great extent the individual comes in contact with the world languages, one reason being that he travels a good deal more than his ancestors. All things considered, modern society is much more complex — because of its pluralistic values and because it offers so many alternatives for thinking and acting.

William Stern once defined intelligence as a general aptitude for adapting cognitively to new tasks, with emphasis on the word 'new'. To that extent people in our time need more ability than ever in order to cope with life. But as the research of most recent decades has shown, ability does not remain static. It can be improved by schooling. The individual who left school at the age of fourteen and his equally intelligent coeval who went on to qualify for university entrance were separated by about 15 IQ points by the time they reached twenty — a difference that could be established from following up a representative group of school pupils in Malmö. However, ability also has to do with motivation and a sense of identity. A person with confidence in his qualifications, and a resolve to use them, achieves more than the one who rightly or wrongly perceives himself to be 'stupid'. Ability implies more than mere adjustment. It also has a 'creative' dimension. It has to do with new 'divergent' thinking and hence also with nonconformism, radicalism and an active quest to change life, not just adapt to it.

It is not my intention here to initiate an inquiry into the 'nature' of ability. My preceding observations should suffice to make it clear that, in a more technical, complex, pluralistic and changeable mass media society, greater demands are put both on passive adjustment and on the ability to find new ways for creativeness. To meet these demands everyone must acquire a broadened liberal education, be equipped with the skills needed to master a register of situations broader than those which an array of routine acts can handle, and obtain a greater grasp of life's different aspects. There will be particular need for more of the learning that tells us how learning can be examined and acquired. Training for specific vocations will lose its relative (though not absolute) importance in a society where tomorrow's economy and the jobs it has to offer can be predicted only in broad outline. The import of a 'learning society' is that more and more people will have to educate themselves for longer periods. That is not only in line with individual interests and democratic fairness, but is also a strong public need at a time when private enterprise has an almost insatiable need for highly skilled manpower and where the individual also counts educational consumption as part of a good living standard.

Higher education in the Soviet Union

It is now in order to say a few words about that variant of the learning society represented by the Soviet Union. The Russian Revolution did away not only with the hereditary aristocracy but also with part of the middle class intelligentsia employed in industry and the professions. In 1918 nearly two-thirds of the adult population was illiterate. For the new regime, therefore, it was a matter not only of building up an educational system for children and young people, but also of creating a system where adults could assiduously improve themselves with night courses and correspondence studies. Many of today's political and industrial leaders, who now make up the new intelligentsia, reached the top through hard work and constant studying. In 1958, when the

Supreme Soviet adopted the new school law,
Khrushchev said that 60 per cent of the students
enrolled in Moscow's higher seats of learning came from
the homes of 'intelligentsia and functionaries'. Two
explanations for this state of affairs suggest themselves:
first, because of centralism, competition to enter these
educational establishments is very keen; and second,
applicants nurtured by parents educated in the first
generation enjoyed an advantage over others.

Truth to tell, higher education in the Soviet Union is
associated not only with prestige and influence, but also
with economic favours. I am reminded of a Finnish
colleague who was invited to spend two weeks as the
guest of the Soviet Academy of Science. An academy vice-
president picked him up and took him to his hotel. He was
instructed that his room would not have to be paid for,
after which he was given a book of coupons to cover his
meals and also an envelope with currency meant to pay for
his other expenses. Objecting that virtually all his
expenses were already covered, he hesitated to take the
money. 'No, it's yours,' said his host, 'you see, here in the
Soviet Union we look after our intellectuals.'

Trends in the United States

A quite different situation in essential respects has evolved
in the other superpower. By 1918 its more advanced
states had implemented eight years of elementary schooling,
and plans were in readiness to extend universal secondary
education in high school up to the age of eighteen, even
though school attendance was compulsory only up to
fifteen or sixteen. At that time the American school was
supposed to perform a twofold mission: it was to
'socialize' the hordes of immigrant children, that is make
Americans of them; and it was to prepare young people
for jobs in an economy that was highly expansive and

industrialized. Only a very small proportion of the cohorts went on to college and university. In effect, education at that level amounted to a status symbol and was considered, as in Europe, to impart social finish to young people from the higher strata.

In an essay of mine published during the 1950s under the title 'Travels in American education', I called attention to the unfathomable inconsistency which held in the US as late as ten years or so ago: namely, the belief in education as all-important for the invididual on the one hand, and on the other hand the low esteem with which teachers were regarded, especially as manifested by the paltry salaries paid to them. The American scale of values long played up the 'self-made man', the newspaper boy who worked his way up to company boss. Intellectuals were clustered at the bottom end of the status scale. The professor was regarded with indulgent smiles. Intellectual achievement was less important than making money. Although social mobility has long been greater in the US than in Europe, it is far from being as great as popular folklore likes to make out.

However, things started changing after 1945. To some extent the change has been impelled by conditions similar to those in the Soviet Union. Scientists and technologists have left their ivory towers to man government departments and the huge federal programmes. Federal spending on research and development was running at an annual rate of more than $15 billion in the mid 1960s; of this sum $4 billion went on basic research, mainly at the universities. It started with the wartime programme of atomic research and continued in the late 1940s with heavy research contracts farmed out by government agencies. As late as the mid-1950s, however, the amounts spent on scientific and technological research were still relatively modest. But for various reasons, among them the belief that research and education make tools for improved international competitiveness and strengthened military potential, resources for research began to overflow all limits. When the National Science Foundation was formed it had a starting budget of $1 million or so. In ten years' time that amount soared to several hundred millions and not only went directly to scientific research, but also boosted it indirectly through the design of material-methods systems for improving school instruction in mathematics, physics, chemistry and biology. Automation and electronics have revolutionized the labour market. It has become very difficult to maintain employment levels for the 'underprivileged': racial minorities or indeed all those with poor grounding in the rudiments. Social and economic planning, formerly regarded with deep distrust, proved to be necessary. For that purpose the federal government had to engage the services of social scientists, especially economists. As computer technology proceeded to mould new patterns of work in factories, offices and laboratories, there arose greater need for the services of other experts, such as programmers and systems men.

The intellectuals – technologists, scientists, 'professors' – have marched into Washington and other places where important activities take place and important decisions are made. Nor is the role of experts necessarily limited to counselling the politicians or broadening their information base; by virtue of the special insights they have into intricate matters, the experts virtually become policymakers themselves. The administration in Washington now employs permanent advisers in science, economics, technology – and, yes, even in education.

The trend towards meritocracy

A similar course of events is discernible in Sweden. It may be of interest to study the role performed by scientists on the important government committees of inquiry, the bodies which so thoroughly prepare the reform programmes in most sectors of Swedish society. As early as the 1930s these committees began to bring in social science expertise on a modest scale. Especially striking was the participation of social scientists in the inquiries which prepared the major reforms in social welfare and education.

The big government research councils all date from 1945. As usual, the first to get their councils and all that money were the physical sciences, engineering and medicine. A social science council came next and eventually a humanistic research council.

The formation of a government research advisory board in 1962 must be seen as reflecting the need felt in government circles to establish direct contacts with exponents of the different disciplines. This body has a secretariat in the Cabinet Office headed by a professor. Different advisory groups, among them one in the economic sphere, have begun to set up headquarters in the government office building. Here it is not so much a question, as is true for the research advisory board, of setting up lines of communication between the political and scientific communities as of providing cabinet ministers with the information they think they need to make their policy decisions.

We need not continue this sweeping discourse save to press home its evidence that we seem indeed to be moving towards growing influence by experts, that is towards increased meritocracy. The influence here involved is at two levels. First, transformation of the economy generates the need to educate the many up to a level previously reserved for an élite few. In sheer numbers, therefore, the society will have more highly educated people than ever before. Second, the rapidly growing top stratum will distil its own élite of experts – eminent scientists, technologists, economists, psychologists and so on – who will increasingly tend to do the research ordered

by the body politic and also to furnish government
agencies and politicians with the advice they feel they
need.

Equal opportunity for all

Education generally, and higher education in particular,
used to be very much a status symbol. It constituted an
integral part of the social class role. The struggle to cast
the compulsory school in a suitable organizational mould
was fought at the superficial level over something called
differentiation. Feelings ran deeper among the opponents
of the comprehensive school system, who argued that it
would alter the status structure. As soon as enrolment in
different kinds of education is no longer a question of
tradition and social background, but rather a question of
rivalry, some will risk losing status by not coming in,
while those who do come in will gain correspondingly.
The people who oppose reforms of the school structure,
whereby educational opportunities are broadened
socially, are usually the same people who adhere to the
theory that the 'talent reservoir' is limited by nature, though
they willingly concede that this intellectual capital has not
been fully utilized so far. Accordingly, it becomes necessary
to search out the relatively few who are born with
promising talents in low-status homes and see to it that
they are enabled to take an advanced education. This
belief has been espoused with special force in England.
Prior to the reform of 1944, the socially exclusive grammar
schools reserved free places for poor boys. In principle, as
many educators hold (and not only in England), mental
ability is inherited. The school – and in particular its
structure – cannot do much about that. Typically, even
The Rise of the Meritocracy, written by a radical British
author, implicitly assumes that every individual is born
with a talent that largely remains unchangeable for life.

In that respect he seems the captive of a notion that has also dominated British psychology, though not usually its politically radical sociology.

The Swedish process of social levelling out and broadening educational opportunities has not been without its elements of drama. In the late 1940s less than 10 per cent of a cohort went on to the *gymnasium*, or pre-university school. Today, 30 per cent go to the *gymnasium* and at least 20 per cent to the institutions which run parallel with it, the continuation school (*fackskola*) and the vocational school (*yrkesskola*). Because of the school reform, the level of expectations has risen dramatically in the space of a few years. As Härnqvist has shown in a comparison between parallel school districts and comprehensive school districts, pupils in the latter have much higher educational ambitions within comparable social categories. This means that the talent reservoir will be better utilized. That in turn implies a greatly increased social mobility, not least for young people from the countryside, at the same time as the whole social system is being changed by shifts in the economy towards occupations which put a premium on highly trained manpower.

The large interest-group associations, especially those which embody popular movements such as the trade unions, used to recruit their officials from the ranks of those who had 'travelled the long road' through diligent self-tuition. Now they increasingly tend to engage people who have already acquired a broad fundamental education. The same holds true for manufacturing and commercial firms, which tend to attach less weight to an applicant's specialized know-how but all the more to whether he has the educational background that lends itself to a broad range of applications, and hence makes him a potential career prospect.

But do not all the measures that have been taken to

confer equal opportunities on one and all in our society
(where education is only one example) suggest that we
are moving towards a levelling out in various respects, for
instance as regards status and pay? Obviously 'equal
opportunity' cannot entail more than a formal equality,
one where everyone is given the same chance to 'line up'.
And once all the contestants are entered in the race, we
cannot thereby assume that they will breast the tape at the
same time. The geneticist Dobzhansky, who has researched
this complex of problems, argues that equal opportunity will
enhance variation precisely because the genetic differences
will then have greater scope for asserting themselves.

Meritocracy: the consequence of a social system

I have tried to avoid taking sides on the value issue: is the
development of society towards meritocracy desirable or
not? Many have adopted lofty tones of moral
condemnation at the prospect of a 'theoretical' imbalance
in the educational system and of tendencies towards
imposing greater demands on basic schooling. Surely no
one is minded to help make society meritocratic if it means
no more than scrambling for marks and sacrificing integrity
for a career. It seems to me that certain politicians, horror-
struck by the insatiable demand for education that has
spread to all sections of the community, have failed to
discover the defective logic of their own preaching. On the
one hand they never tire of upholding education together
with research as the most dynamic factor in our society.
On the other hand, when they see the many young people
who want to enter our *gymnasiums* and universities, they
say that the value of education is overrated. Indeed, they
have even intimated that instruments of wage policy should
be deployed to make education less attractive, convinced
that most people seek a better education in order to fatten
their purses.

Meritocracy is not something we are free to take or leave irrespective of the society in which it functions. It is an integral part of the social system where education and the use of talents are the very determinants of economic growth. Hence meritocracy, as I see it, is a factor thrown into the price we must pay for a higher standard of living. It forms part of the quest for a 'better' society in the material sense. Meritocracy is intertwined with the whole value system that sustains thinking on economic growth. It then also becomes a sacrifice on the altar of welfare and affluence. Some of the more articulate young people who come from homes where the parents have done well socially, from families who have cars, second homes and who often travel abroad, have increasingly begun to question the 'sense' of scrambling for marks and seeking for status. Is it a better material standard that is needed, or something else? That is the ultimate question which the meritocracy debate will have to answer.

The place of comparative and international education in the education of teachers[1]

Whatever criteria we employ, we shall find that both comparative and international education have emerged as disciplines in their own right since 1945. Educational issues since then have rapidly moved up to the international level. Before then they were treated as local, provincial or at most national problems. International co-operation, interchange of experiences, and technical assistance to developing countries now occur on a scale that would have been inconceivable twenty-five years ago. This tremendous change stems from several causes of which the following seem to me to be the most important.

When economists in highly industrialized countries began to show (or think that they had shown) that education was more than mere consumption – that it also accounted for a considerable portion of economic growth – national and international bodies were spurred to invest more in education in both advanced and developing countries in order to boost the economic growth rate. Thus, for instance, the Organization for Economic Co-operation and Development (OECD) since its policy conference in

[1] Invited paper presented at the World Congress of Comparative Education Societies in Ottawa, Canada, 20 August 1970.

Washington DC in 1961 has devoted increasing efforts in
its member countries to investigations of how the
the productivity of the educational systems can be
enhanced in order to achieve an increased economic
growth. The World Bank has begun to give high priority
to loans to school systems in developing countries.

Education is more and more regarded as a 'propelling
force' in modern society as well as an outcome of a higher
standard of living. Thus, education is both partly cause and
partly effect in the intricate fabric of social change. The
founding of an organization like UNESCO was
accompanied by great expectations as to what education
could accomplish in the world's developing areas. At
conferences organized by UNESCO in Addis Ababa and
Karachi, highly ambitious targets were set for the
elimination of illiteracy in Africa and Asia. These targets
have since been scaled down to more realistic levels as a
result of, among other things, education, particularly
formal education, not only having produced social and
economic changes but also – perhaps to a larger extent –
being a consequence of them. During the 1960s this
insight was instrumental in giving birth to a new discipline
– educational planning, with special application to
developing countries. Educational planning represents a
confluence of theory and empirical findings from
comparative education, economics, demography,
anthropology and the history of education.

Due to greater geographic mobility and the expansion of
markets and means of communication, an increased
international exchange of students has occurred, for the
most part at the university level but to no small extent
in secondary schooling as well. By the end of the 1960s
more than 100,000 foreign students were enrolled at
American universities. The figure for Europe was roughly
75,000. More and more young people are taking studies
abroad in a language other than their mother tongue.

Indeed, we are heading for an internationalized world where a large segment of education will have to cross frontiers in order to make it serviceable. This is especially true for young people from small countries.

In response to a mounting need to establish international standards for the evaluation of the quality of degrees and diplomas and proficiency in specific subjects, various new initiatives have been taken. There is a strong need to establish international standards at the pre-university level in order to make it easier for institutions of higher learning to evaluate the qualifications attained in the secondary academic school in one system in terms of another country's requirements. Under a grant from the Ford Foundation an attempt is under way by a project group in Geneva to establish requirements for an 'international baccalaureate'. A similar project has been launched in Belgium. The research initiated ten years ago by the International Association for the Evaluation of Educational Achievement (IEA) emerged partly in this context. One by-product of IEA surveys in mathematics, science and other subject areas has been to define operationally and more exactly international performance standards by devising international tests based upon analyses of national curricula and work carried out by international expert committees.

Comparative education has evolved as a fully fledged discipline only since 1945. Before then it was (and still is to some extent) mainly addressed to general descriptions of educational systems in different countries and to the juxtaposition of these descriptions. Nowadays greater scope is given to analyses which permit generalizations as to how various social, economic and pedagogic factors shape educational systems. Countries differ from one another in terms of school structure, curricula and methods of instruction. They also differ in terms of the socio-politico-economic matrix in which the school system operates. Since many of the factors on both the 'input' and 'output' side vary more between than within countries, an international analysis permits a better grasp of what 'produces' a certain educational outcome than an analysis confined to one national system only. Comparative education also provides an opportunity to replicate studies in different national settings and thereby to arrive at generalizations which could not be drawn from single country studies.

I think that this background should be kept in mind when we set out to discuss the proper role of comparative and international education in teacher training. Even in a world of self-contained countries without international migration and exchange, comparative education would, of course, just as the history and philosophy of education do, contribute to give the teacher a better and more detached perspective on his own educational system and thereby on his task. But with rapidly increased internationalization, not least in terms of making professional training marketable outside the particular country where the prospective teacher happened to be trained, one could indeed make a case for a thorough course in comparative education with tangible and pragmatic objectives. However, we cannot expect a teaching candidate to become a better classroom instructor in terms of being able to impart knowledge more efficiently just because he has taken courses in comparative education. The same would of course apply to the study of the history or the philosophy of education. But the evaluation of teacher training programmes suggests that even such a highly tangible area as educational psychology does not seem to bear any conclusive relationship to short-range criteria of teaching competence.

Nevertheless, we have not allowed these negative findings to discourage us to the extent of abolishing such courses in education. In spite of everything, we hope, and sometimes even take for granted, that certain academic coursework in education will have long-range effects in terms of affecting the prospective teacher's frame of mind, his attitude and general outlook in a way that is conducive to, for instance, increased international understanding and heightened readiness to accept innovations.

Let me try to be a little bit more specific and spell out what I think that a course in comparative education should aim at achieving.

(1) The overriding objective should be to open the student's perspective and to prevent the ethnocentric provincialism that often prevails among educators, particularly when it comes to evaluating students from other systems. By learning about other educational systems the teaching candidate is brought to regard the world as a big educational laboratory in which highly different structural and pedagogical practices are employed. The mere juxtaposition of the various systems can contribute to a more relativistic and less dogmatic attitude towards educational practices. Thus comparative education contributes to broadening the perspective on educational issues, as the teaching of the history and philosophy of education similarly does. It thereby also contributes to achieving international understanding in an era of rapidly increased international contacts.

(2) Comparative education should contribute to a deeper understanding of how the educational systems operate within the greater framework of the socio-politico-economic systems at large. One is repeatedly struck by the fact that educators tend to conceive of education as if it operated in a social vacuum. This one experiences so frequently that one is led to believe that it is a kind of professional disease. An illustration might suffice in this connection. The problem of structural change from a selective and dualistic system

to a comprehensive and unitary one in several countries in Western Europe has, as you all know, been accompanied by rather heated debate. On the part of the educators the argument has almost throughout been confined to the pedagogic sphere. Up to what age is it possible to keep the 'academic' and 'practical' pupils together in the same classroom? To what extent will the able pupils be hampered by their less able classmates? Rather seldom does one find in educational circles attempts to judge the merits or drawbacks of the two systems in terms of social and economic factors. When Jackson carried out his study of streaming in England and assessed the teachers' opinions of it, he found that the great majority were in favour of this practice because of its supposed pedagogic merits. The bright pupils could move ahead and the dull ones did not have to become discouraged by the presence of their more successful age-mates.

(3) Comparative education, at least when based upon cross-national empirical data, can help us to kill quite a lot of educational folklore. Particularly in times of crisis there is a tendency to pass judgement on the relative merits of various systems and/or practices on the basis of extremely thin evidence, and as a last resort recourse is taken to pure folklore. The reaction in the United States after the first sputnik is a case in point. Soon after the launching a stream of American educators began breathlessly to head for the Soviet Union. What had previously been close to high treason now suddenly began to be regarded as the highest virtue. Prestige figures started to compare education in the United States with that in the European countries. Admiral Rickover maintained that the educational system in old imperial Germany was so good that it was copied in many places and still deserved to be emulated. One could not avoid wondering how the

German *humanistisches Gymnasium* would have been able to produce among other things the technologists and scientists that Rickover maintained were so badly needed in order to build submarines. It is typical of quite a lot of the comparative judgements passed on the quality of education in various countries that comparisons are made between the end products, i.e. graduating students, without the slightest thought about how many of a given pool of students have been brought so far. The price paid for the quality, in terms of grade-repeating and drop-out, is very seldom taken into account. Almost never are the social and economic implications and consequences of a certain structural set-up or a certain curriculum considered.

So far, I have stated objectives which are common to all national teacher education, irrespective of whether it is pre-service or in-service education. But during the last two decades there has been a growing need for a pool of international educators, suitable for work particularly in developing countries. In order to train them properly, one has to emphasize their social role as promoters of change rather than their role as transmitters of knowledge. The urgent need to provide professional training of educators qualified for work in international assistance training programmes has been met by courses organized at universities in several countries. Educators who take assignments in developing countries or otherwise go in for international work should learn to look upon educational systems as integral parts of socioeconomic and cultural systems. Such a training has to a very large extent to be cross-disciplinary. It has as a rule postgraduate status with advanced degrees granted on the basis of courses completed in comparative education, sociology, anthropology and economics.

How then, should we try to achieve the objectives of comparative education outlined above?

(1) I cannot see how we could possibly avoid the traditional lecture course in comparative education plus the assigned reading. Now, and in the foreseeable future, reading books and being stimulated (hopefully) by somebody commenting upon them is still the main road to insights. This does not prevent us from improving our traditional courses in comparative education. Quite a lot of them, I suspect, have been rather dull, not least because of the tremendous amount of badly structured descriptive information they have tried to convey.

(2) A certain amount of what sometimes in a derogatory way is referred to as 'educational tourism' could be helpful. By seeing for oneself, i.e. by visiting schools and talking to teachers in other countries, a more concrete picture can be obtained.

(3) A more advanced type of 'educational tourism' is represented by teacher exchange. The main problem in expanding the existing programme has not been one of differences in curricula between countries, but simply one of language difficulties. Language teachers from countries where none of the main world languages are spoken could not take exchange assignments in for instance English- or French-speaking countries since they are not trained in other subject areas such as science or social studies.

For various reasons it seems more fruitful to put greater emphasis on comparative education in in-service instead of pre-service training. During the pre-service training the prospective teacher's mind is primarily preoccupied with problems of classroom management, discipline and methods of instruction, so that comparative education and related areas of education as a discipline seem rather irrelevant to his classroom task.

What should be the proper outline of a syllabus in comparative education? It would be preposterous if I tried to be very specific here for the simple reason that my experience is too limited.

(1) If we want to convey to the students how education is related to economic and social change, it is advantageous if the course in comparative education is planned in close co-operation with the ones in educational sociology and the history of education. Topics where such a co-operation would seem to be fruitful are for example the emerging elementary education in Western Europe and how it is related to industrialization, polytechnic education in the Soviet Union or the role of the school as an agent of Americanization in the USA. A case study which hopefully could convey a deeper understanding of the socioeconomic relationship is provided by Japanese educational development.

(2) The final aim in teaching comparative education, as has been emphasized several times, is to bring about a deeper understanding of the factors moulding the educational systems. Therefore efforts should be made to avoid the abundance of more or less unstructured descriptive material which make some texts in comparative education resemble canned food. Descriptive material has of course to be presented but it has to be made available under such headings as make it ready not only for juxtaposition but also for closer analysis.

One major topical area is represented by the organizational structures in terms of types of schools covering certain ages and certain grades. In order to understand structures one also ought to know about admissions, enrolments and transfers from one stage or one type to another. A study of current structural change in Europe could profit highly by focusing on the problems of selective versus comprehensive education. In this connection particular attention has to be given to the relation between education and social mobility. Admission to the university-preparing secondary schools and to the universities themselves is another area with quite a lot of interesting social problems related to education. I have found that comparisons between countries in terms of grade-repeating and drop-out rates are highly conducive to further inquiry. This also applies to statistics about how various socioeconomic groups are represented in academic secondary schools and at universities.

The curricular problems pertaining to subject areas, number of hours of instruction and, not least, outlines of syllabuses could serve as means of achieving an undogmatic state of mind in looking at educational problems. Not infrequently syllabuses in one's own country are looked upon as though they were metaphysically given. To change them is therefore sacrilege.

Administration and the decision-making process, both that which entails long-range policy making and that which concerns the day-to-day operations of an educational system, is another area which also can lead to fruitful discussion and thereby to deeper understanding of the role of education in the society of today.

For a long time we badly needed suitable texts, both those which focused on a systematic presentation of facts about structure, enrolment, curriculum, etc. and those which tried to present comparative education as a structured discipline. Descriptive material collated by organizations like UNESCO, the Council of Europe and the OECD has been made available in impressive publications. But the material going into these publications is based upon information obtained from the ministries of education or other official agencies. As a rule it has to be cleared through the respective governments before publication. In many cases more reliable material could have been obtained from other sources. This does not necessarily imply that material included in the publications referred to is faked but simply that there is difficulty in establishing strict comparability. We still lack an international terminology which would be lead to more adequate comparisons at the pure descriptive-statistical level. In recent years a series of texts, such as the ones by Bereday, Noah and Eckstein, and Coombs, have become available for teaching undergraduate courses in comparative education in a more systematic and integrated way. In all three cases referred to the authors have been able to get away from the pure descriptive approach and aim at a deeper understanding, by taking into account the social and economic dimensions of the educational systems.

For a long time the descriptive historico-philosophical approach prevailed in the teaching of comparative education. Students have had to read texts describing the education in one country after another, sometimes with comments on the historical background and its relationship to current religious and philosophical beliefs. The present trend is to make comparative education more empirical and thereby to bring it into closer contact with the social sciences. Such a trend is promoted by the attempts to measure educational outcomes in terms of international standards. It is also inspired by experience gained in providing technical assistance in education where efficiency has to go hand in hand with attempts to seek hard facts.

The time has passed when a teacher is trained merely in order to fit a closely circumscribed national system of education. In a shrinking world, teaching skills and related

competencies will have to be made transferable and
available for international use. The time might come
sooner than we can imagine when massive transfer of
teachers from developed to developing countries takes
place. In a shrinking world, teacher education must break
its provincialism and open up international perspectives.
Comparative education could certainly be instrumental in
achieving this.

Research and innovation   3

The limitations of experiments in education

Educational research has long been confronted with a
double dilemma. Over the past few decades it has amassed
a vast amount of descriptive material, yet a mere handful
of generally valid conclusions have been producible from
all this abundance. It has come up with some very useful
findings on the 'ambiance' of education, for example, in
matters relating to scholastic aptitude, achievements and
social background, but has a meagre record of performance
on the central issue, i.e. the teaching and learning process
in the classroom itself.

The attempts at theory-building and research design
which have been instrumental in transforming education
from an art into a science are really not much more than
ten years old. Much of the spur to this development has
come from the advent of new technical aids such as
internal television (ITV) and videotape recording, which has
permitted studies of the teaching process that were not
technically feasible earlier. At Stanford University, for
example, R. Bush, N. L. Gage, D. Allen and F. McDonald
have drawn on ITV to develop an improved system of
teacher training, at the same time as they have identified

important dimensions of teacher behaviour and sought
to relate these to learning by pupils.

Thinking on methodological questions, as well as
research on them, has long been muddled by not keeping
teaching and learning separate. What the pupils learn is
supposed to be determined almost entirely by the
instruction actually communicated. Hence 'good' and 'bad'
learning by pupils is assumed to reflect 'good' and 'bad'
teaching. As is well known, a great deal of learning takes
place in spite of bad teaching because the stimuli of tests,
homework and the like can get pupils to learn much outside
the classroom, for example, through the efforts of parents.
Conversely, 'good' teaching can lead to poor results by
virtue of circumstances inside and outside the school over
which the teacher has no control.

In recent years researchers such as N. L. Gage,
J. Stanley and D. Campbell, in trying to develop paradigms
for the performance of educational experiments, have
identified the attendant difficulties and sources of error.
The discourse which follows will recapitulate a few
problems of experimental method in education.

Experimental difficulties

The natural sciences have long since developed an
experimental method with good results. This has gone
hand in hand with an inductive logic that is used to draw
generalizable conclusions from the phenomena under
study. It is therefore natural for the modern social sciences
to have looked up to their older cousin as an example
worth following. Hence the widespread belief that the
shaping of education would be amenable to the same
process of experimentation that has contributed so much to
today's industrial technology. A very strong influence was
exerted on the social sciences, not least education, by
R. A. Fisher with his rules on the conclusions to be drawn

from different 'treatments', based on the statistical methods
developed in agricultural research. Some quarters have
found it axiomatic that the most sophisticated type of
educational research is the experimental design, since it
permits conclusions as to what causes what. Should I
wish to try out a new method of teaching children the
fundamental concepts of numbers, I can randomly divide
a sufficiently large group of them into experimental and
control classes. To be on the safe side, the starting position
of the children in different respects should be examined.
Their retention of subject matter must be determined
without fail when the experimental period ends.
Differences which fall outside the framework of chance,
i.e. statistically significant differences between those
taught with the 'new' method and those taught with the
'conventional' method, are ascribed to the dissimilarity of
'treatment', in this case the methods of instruction applied.
In principle, then, the same kind of design is involved as in
a study concerned with the effects of different fertilizers.

When carrying out an educational experiment one deals
with various 'input' factors which are studied for their
influence on the 'output' factors, i.e. the knowledge
retained. To resort to the conventional jargon, one deals
with a series of independent and dependent variables.
Generally speaking, it is easier to measure the dependent
variables, the outcome of teaching. But even that can be
difficult enough, especially if the investigator is also
fired with an ambition to measure some of the more
imponderable factors, such as attitudes to a subject,
cognitive style and ability to think in the concepts and
principles of the subject. As a rule, the difficulties posed by
the independent side are even greater. In the first place,
the conditions determining the educational processes are
many and complicated; second, the independent factors
that lack relevance for the particular experiment must be
kept under control.

Most of the educational experiments are marred by one or more of the following defects. There is all the more reason to pinpoint them because they are usually overlooked, even in the handbooks.

The use of a certain 'method' in teaching must not – and cannot – be equated with use of a certain fertilizer. The latter has a known and exact chemical composition, and hence a maximum consistency, whereas an educational 'method' bears a label that covers an enormous diversity of systematic approaches and procedures. Take a random selection of scientific monographs on educational experiments, and you will find them tediously belabouring one point: the 'new' method does not yield significantly better (or worse) results than the 'conventional' method. However, both types of 'treatment', the conventional as well as the experimental, are marked by a vast heterogeneity. Not only that, but the teachers assigned to experimental and control classes usually represent a small – and in most cases a highly unsatisfactory – sample of the instructional procedures employed. Owing to the great variation in methodology, it is highly probable that the two 'treatments' largely overlap, which means that no statistically significant difference between them can in fact arise. There simply is no such thing as *the* conventional' teaching, no more than there is *the* 'activating' or 'individualizing' version. This also explains why so many of the experiments made with television have failed to produce results that significantly differ from other modes of instruction. Instruction by TV does not represent a homogeneous method, but covers a vast array of procedures in which TV is used as an aid.

Another basic defect is that the different methods of instruction whose effects one wants to study are not independent of one another. That is particularly true in cases where the same teachers are assigned to both experimental and control classes. A pedagogue who wilfully denies the members of his control classes that which is deemed advantageous for the experimental classes must be a *rara avis* indeed. But even in cases where different teachers are assigned to each type of class, it stands to reason that they will communicate not only methodological ideas but also, and more important, expectations of results from the experiment.

A third difficulty has to do with interaction between the independent variables. These are of four kinds: attributes of the pupils (e.g. scholastic ability and school motivation), attributes of the 'material' educational situation (e.g. size of class and availability of aids), attributes of the teacher (e.g. attitudes to the pupils and to the degree of control to impose) and attributes of the subject matter (e.g. subject field and mode of presentation). The interaction manifests itself as correlations both within the different groups of variables and between these groups. The interaction between teacher, pupil and method has several implications, among them that a given method of instruction will have different effects according to the attributes of pupil, teacher and subject.

As I noted earlier, these difficulties for the strict application of experimental approaches to educational research are usually overlooked. A review of recent literature in this field discloses that experiments performed with a handful of teachers are accepted as satisfactory, provided only that the pupils have been randomly distributed among the different class categories. Which gives cause for asking: would it not be more fruitful scientifically to conduct a survey of a large number of *actually* existing classes, where the breadth of variation in method is representatively mirrored, rather than make do with a few teachers whose methodical variants usually elude all control?

It would take me too far afield to dwell here at any length on the method of multivariate analysis to interpret the outcome of educational studies, whether these be of the experimental or survey type. A nagging doubt that has emerged in the more recent behavioural-science literature is whether the paradigms, which once proved their excellence in research on seed dressings and fertilizers, are applicable in the same way to living objects represented by pupils and teachers.

The role of research in teacher education[1]

The role of teacher training in educational innovation

In terms of its objectives, organization and work practices, the school tends to be highly institutionalized. That also applies to the institutions for the training of teachers. It may well be asked whether these institutions are not more conservative in certain respects and more incapable of adapting to the new conditions than the schools out in the field. Whereas a consensus has largely prevailed within the Swedish political community with regard to those changes of school organization that have been made during the last two decades, large groups of secondary school teachers have opposed these structural changes. Most of the arguments advanced for the organizational changes have been social, with reference made to new societal needs and equality of educational opportunity; most of the arguments against them have been pedagogical. Those who have opposed adjustments of the school to new social determinants have implicitly reasoned as though the school's objectives and work practices were largely unrelated to the societal framework. This applied to some

[1] Paper presented at the 5th General Conference of the Comparative Education Society in Europe, in Stockholm, 18 June 1971.

secondary school teachers, for example, when the debate on so-called differentiation at the upper level of the compulsory school was at its liveliest.

A central issue for the teacher training institutions is how to go about introducing the *innovations* of course content and – above all – work practices, which are necessary prerequisites to enable the school to adjust adequately to the radical new conditions emerging in a changing society. Teacher education must not become a conserving element of the school system, with generation after generation of educators teaching time-honoured and unchallenged patent methods. The teacher training institutions must be designed so as to foster the spirit of inquiry and experimentation, as well as undogmatic criticism of the established order – a prerequisite for introducing needed changes in the school.

Teacher education can be given a 'strategic' position in this innovation process, partly by spearheading the development of methods of instruction, and partly by arrangements both in teacher education and the in-service training to ensure that the results of development work are disseminated and implemented in practice.

According to the curriculum studies conducted by the Stockholm School of Education for the 1957 Swedish Governmental School Commission and the Industrial Council for Social and Economic Studies, a considerable discrepancy was found between curricular prescriptions and actual classroom practice with regard to course content and work practices. Whereas the prescriptions gave fairly 'progressive' directions for the teaching of Swedish, for example, the actual teaching adhered for the most part to the instructional plan of 1919.

It is not my intention here to analyse either the determinants of the school of today or the altered demands that this has imposed on the teachers. The goals of teacher education have been thoroughly discussed in other

contexts. It should suffice for present purposes to single
out the following factors:

(1) More and more young people are staying on in school
for longer periods (this is the familiar 'educational
explosion'). As a result the school must now take care
of *all* kinds and degrees of abilities. There is no longer
any question of the school being called upon to cull an
élite. The object is to make the most of everyone's
potential as far as possible, which in principle signifies
a radical individualization.

(2) The 'knowledge explosion' denotes a shift away from
the encyclopedic, knowledge-storing ideal of education
towards the acquisition of skills: included here is the
ability to think in those categories which characterize
a certain discipline and the ability to solve problems
in the subject field on one's own. The intellectual diet
that the school can give its pupils does not provide
sufficient nourishment. This observation applies with
even greater force to the efforts made by the teacher
training institutions.

(3) Research in the behavioural and social sciences and the
advent of new technical aids are bound to react on the
organization of work and on work practices in the
school. In these latter respects the school is still very
much at the pre-industrial stage.

Measures which promote innovations in the school

As already observed, the teacher training institutions enjoy
a strategic position in the work of educational development,
a position which follows from their training of new teachers
as well as from their assistance in the further education of
already practising teachers. If these institutions were to
take little or no part in this work they would readily
become a conserving element in the school system. The
impulses to renewal would then come from other quarters.

If the teacher training institutions are to become a force for progress in the school's reform work, the following conditions must be met:

(1) Research into problems that are thrust up by the continuing work of educational reform should be pursued *in close contact* with teacher education itself. For this purpose the contact must not be restricted to orienting student teachers and teacher trainers to the methods and results of research; instead, these groups should be actively involved in the research work. That applies in particular to the teacher trainers.

(2) Every teacher training institution ought to be equipped with a *laboratory school for experiments and demonstrations.* Such a facility, which should be of moderate size, must not be used for practice teaching but, as the name suggests, serve two purposes, namely (1) to constitute an experimental school, where new types of teaching, methods and aids are tested on a trial basis; and (2) to give student teachers the opportunities to observe children more systematically than is possible in the normal school setting and – even more important – to enable the students to see sophisticated work practices in concrete use.

(3) The methods teachers should be actively involved in the research and development (R and D) work that is carried on in the laboratory school. When instructing in their subject they must be enabled to show concrete manifestations of the new methodological tools as well as to analyse their background more systematically. It follows that the posts of methods teachers should be shaped so as to give the incumbent considerable latitude to take part in the work of developing new methods of instruction. It may therefore be asked whether every methods teacher should not at some

time in his career be assigned to a graduate school of education, so as to work closely with the educational researchers.

By taking steps to put methods teachers – and, for that matter, supervisors of student teaching as well – in daily contact with the educational R and D work, either through their own active efforts or by enabling them to collaborate with those who continuously have to tackle the problems, the result will be to create, if not guarantee, conditions at least more favourable than exist now for them to spearhead the work of methods development within the school.

With the measures outlined above, contact with scientific research in the school sector would help impart a more undogmatic climate to teacher education, deflate the cocksureness identified with training colleges and encourage greater receptiveness to innovations. There would be less danger of teaching becoming petrified in patented routines. Research may be expected to produce these effects not only on the strength of its findings but also – and perhaps chiefly – by subjecting problems to debate by casting doubt on the axiomatic, on that which has been held to be self-evident and thoroughly confirmed by all so-called experience. The adjustment of teacher education to constantly changing determinants in the school system, and the conduct of R and D programmes that can provide the school with adequate tools, will stand or fall with the extent to which education takes place in that spirit of inquiry which permeates all research work and is the quintessence of higher learning.

Research and development projects

As a matter of course, the R and D pursued in connection with teacher education would have to tackle key problems in the practical sphere, not least those which are brought to the fore by educational reforms. Emphasis should therefore be put on applied, i.e. decision-oriented, research. It is assumed that basic research, particularly in the behavioural or social sciences, of relevance to the educational sphere will have to be pursued in large part at other institutions, for instance the institutions of experimental psychology, statistics and sociology. But here, no less than in other sectors, the distinction between basic and applied research should not be drawn too hard and fast. A project that aims at a very specific target often gives rise to new methodological problems of the greatest importance for basic research. The same holds true for the results of applied research. A couple of examples may be cited. The standard tests used for equalization purposes in certain grades of the comprehensive school were for some time developed at the Stockholm school of education. Their actual construction generated various methodological problems especially with regard to determining the reliability of the tests used. The analysis of these problems has been very important for the theory of educational measurement, and has indirectly conferred benefits on the theory's concrete application. Data collected for entire school grades have permitted the special study of large populations of twins, which has resulted in new methods for shedding light on the heredity–environment problem. Another example: representative data have been collected whereby the intellectual development of boys and girls at certain age levels can be subjected to exhaustive investigation.

The following problem areas must be considered central to research into practical education, namely

(1) the objectives and content of teaching
(2) the didactic principles that are most conducive to learning and
(3) the evaluation of outcomes of teaching by objective methods.

Objectives and course content have been successfully
illuminated with scientific methods in the past. Cases in
point are the curriculum studies that were carried out by
the Stockholm school of education in conjunction with
the work of the 1957 Governmental School Commission
and the 1960 Commission of Inquiry into the
pre-university school (*gymnasium*). The latter body came to
base a considerable part of its curriculum recommendations
on the research findings obtained. Considering that
curricula in a changing society continuously have to be
revised, it is necessary to endow curriculum research with
permanent institutional resources so that it can be
continuously maintained. Since it is worthwhile to have
this work carried on in close contact and collaboration
with experts on subject methods, it should be sited at the
teacher training institutions.

Systematic try-out experiments are required to underpin
the development work that relates to methods and teaching
aids. These experiments should, with the assistance of the
methods teacher concerned in their 'exploratory', preparatory
phase, be conducted at the 'experimentation and
demonstration' laboratory schools referred to above. This
field of work is large enough to warrant the operation of
many such laboratory schools, preferably one at each
teacher training institution. As soon as the laboratory
schools have completed the preliminaries, experiments on
a bigger scale can be undertaken 'out in the field', that is,
in ordinary schools.

To the extent that schooling is considered an investment,
there arises the need to *evaluate the effect* of invested
resources. Since a scarcity of teachers and physical plant
must be reckoned with for the foreseeable future, a great
deal of effort will have to be put into investigations which
seek to explain the conditions under which the effect of
resources can be optimized. Since any reform of a specific
grade level touches off a debate as to the appropriate

length of schooling or the volume of instruction that should be given in a specific subject, an investigator must find out what relations exist between age, maturity and length of schooling on the one hand, and the outcomes of teaching on the other.

Theory and practice in teacher education

When the 1946 School Commission submitted its report on the first school of education in 1952 to the Minister of Education, it recommended providing for a new professorship in a subject called 'school research'. The incumbent of this chair would be responsible for the teaching of educational foundation courses both in the regular undergraduate curriculum and in connection with in-service training, where the new school was envisaged as playing a leading role. He would also see to it that instruction in psychology and education tied in closely with research in the area, especially with research that related to experimental programmes. As envisaged by the commission, this post would emphasize research over teaching duties.

Several arguments have been advanced in support of the thesis that educational research ought to be pursued in institutional integration with teacher education, both in the undergraduate phase and in in-service training. Mention has already been made of the concentration on problems that have to do with school reform. It goes without saying that decisions taken by parliament with regard to the organization of the school, as well as the schedules, syllabuses and directives issued by the authorities, will have extremely limited impact on the school's internal work unless the teachers can be actively motivated to explore new paths and aim at new objectives.

It has repeatedly been observed that the potential for reshaping the school will greatly depend on the extent to

which teacher education can be reformed. This is not only
a matter of inculcating new methods of teaching but also
of providing a body of facts that carry conviction. The
researchers are enabled by their work to keep in first-hand
touch with innovations in this sector. It lies in the nature of
research to be pioneering: efforts are made to elucidate
factors that were formerly disregarded or kept dark. It is
vital to imbue the student teachers with a measure of this
pioneering and inquiring spirit. Anyone who has helped
to discover facts finds it easier to abandon erroneous and
biased notions and practices – in short, to change his
attitudes. That cause will be further fostered if the student
teachers take part in the institute's research work, even if
no more than modestly. The Swedish School Commission
in 1952 held out the vision that this would take place to a
fairly considerable extent. But experience has shown that
the curriculum as a whole is such heavy going that the
students cannot devote very much of their undergraduate
time to pursuing their own inquiries or taking part in the
research work at the school of education's Institute of
Education and Research. Some of the students, particularly
those who plan to pursue graduate work, gathered data
for the study of didactic questions in the course of their
practice-teaching terms.

Further, one should not overlook the value of permitting
research to fertilize teacher education with its inquiring
and undogmatic outlook. A great deal of practical teacher
training consists in learning certain rules of thumb. The
risk here is for a student to make do with the 'handlebars'
he has once learned in the belief that these form the very
essence of educational wisdom. One way of trying to
neutralize this risk is to let a bit of the researcher's healthy
scepticism permeate the instruction. One advantage of
getting the student teacher to take a sceptical view of most
things in the educational world is that he will not tend as
readily to regard himself as a 'finished product', which will

make him more receptive to impulses to keep on educating himself.

It is of great importance that those responsible for research at the school of education have a certain teaching contact with the undergraduate students, such that these will be given certain lectures, particularly with reference to research projects relating to school reform.

The educational researchers at the school of education have considered it extremely important to establish co-operation with teachers in methods as well as with supervisor teachers in the laboratory school. This co-operation has been established in various situations and in different forms. Many teachers of methodology attend seminars which deal with the department's own research projects as well as with those undertaken in quest of a doctorate. In connection with planning the curriculum studies referred to earlier, the methods specialists in both elementary and secondary education were actively engaged. Their efforts went into the analyses of existing syllabuses and the wording of the questionnaire that was used to map out actual course content and methods of instruction.

There has also been fruitful co-operation between the educational researchers and the supervisors of student teaching in the design of standardized achievement tests. It started out by going at length into the objectives of teaching in the subject concerned. The next step was to discuss the selection of suitable test material to measure different topics of a subject area. Only then could work commence on the 'authorship' of test problems. In that work the experience of subject experts and able teachers was of the utmost value. As a valuable by-product, it became possible to crystallize and examine the syllabuses in a quite different way from before; the approach taken here was to determine the extent to which the syllabuses squared with the generally expressed objectives of teaching in the subject concerned.

It would have been desirable to extend the co-operation between educational theorists and practicians to embrace other aspects. In the opinion of many, the weakness that has long attached to teacher education is the inadequate co-ordination of the theoretical foundations in psychology and education with methods and teaching practices. It should be considered extremely important to have all three actors in teacher education – professors of education, methods specialists and supervisors – share the same frame of reference, so that they look upon school problems more or less similarly, or at least understand one another's viewpoints. Failing that, there is the risk that they will not talk the same language, which is bound to have a confusing effect on the students. Obviously the advice on general methods which comes from the supervisor in the laboratory school, or the specific pointers related to a particular subject area given by the professor of methodology, will have to be rationally justifiable with reference to more general psychological and pedagogical principles. For that to happen it will be necessary for both supervisors and teachers of methodology to grasp certain fundamentals of educational theory and also to have close contact with those teachers who impart the subject matter. Unless that is sufficiently the case, it is only too likely that instruction in theory will be perceived to bear slightly, not to say dubiously, on the realities of practical education.

Another form of co-operation between teachers of education, researchers, supervisors and teachers of methods is to let the students know, when they pursue their own small research projects or field investigations, that they can also count on assistance from the methods teachers. It must be stressed that instruction in methods should not be restricted to the communication of manual artifices. It is important to subject the methods to investigations of a more scientific and systematic character. That is the only way to guarantee the promotion of a rational development in the didactic field. These self-evident observations by no means imply a degrading of the instruction in practical methods and the broad experience on which this is based, but only a reminder of the need to test the validity of everyday experience with the help of instruments from the armoury of science.

The researcher, not least the one who pursues lines of inquiry in those social sciences whose results have applications for the larger community, often has reason to ask himself: what 'good' will come from all my pains? If he is completely shut up in his ivory tower, he can derive satisfaction from having helped to map out new areas, from having discovered new laws and principles or, in his efforts to solve problems, from having hit upon new methods with apparent promise for further scientific use. Society must accept such basic research without casting anxious side glances at the 'practical' applications. There is a good reason for this: we can never predict with any great accuracy what will be solid ground in the future for building up the scientific edifice.

There is a fruitful interplay between basic and applied research. Time and again a project launched out of sheer curiosity, simply in order to find out more about something, has led to discoveries and findings whose practical application was neither intended nor even dreamt of by the researcher. Conversely, the focus on applied research has often given rise to problems that suggest themselves for basic inquiry or has led on to methods that have significantly borne on the further development of theoretical models.

For natural reasons the educational researcher cannot sit permanently in his ivory tower – though at times sheer fatigue may make him wish for periods when he could hang out the 'Do not disturb' sign. Most of his problems crop up in practical life situations, not least in that of the school. His methods have to be tested out in the field. His facts are gathered in the classrooms, and the sustaining power of his results will sometimes be applied and put to the test in the school's everyday reality. Yet he stands outside the ivory tower in another respect as well. The problems he is assigned to investigate are often controversial, being loaded with the dynamite of professional and scholastic politics. This means that the researcher readily gets caught in the crossfire between interested organizations and pressure groups. Since he cannot afford to align himself with either party, or display either a black or white coat of arms, he risks being squeezed between both sides. Fortunately he need expose himself to that predicament only in the more exceptional cases. It also happens that he will be brought into the decision-making arena if his results influence the school's practice or the acts of educational authorities.

3 Strategies of educational innovation

The study of the innovative process and of the factors conducive to innovation is a fairly new undertaking, less than fifteen years old. I cannot remember that I ever heard the word 'innovation' being used in an educational context until about seven years ago. I take it that the term has been taken over by the educators from industrial technology, as has the entire conception of research and development as part of the implementation of innovative change. Sometimes innovation is preached with a fervour as if it represented a value per se. People are oblivious of the self-evident fact that significant innovations and persistent changes in education ought to represent adequate responses to fundamental transformations in culture and society. Far from all the changes or innovations in education, however, can be regarded as fitting responses to these transformations.

I need not spell out for what reasons it would be appropriate to talk about a 'great mutation' when we are trying to describe the rapid transformation that our societies are at present undergoing. The same applies to certain aspects of our educational systems, such as enrolments and organizations, whereas others are strikingly lagging behind. To put it briefly, what are needed today are strategies whereby applicable knowledge and techniques can be incorporated into the content and organization of curriculum, the methods and materials of instruction and the procedures by which the educational enterprise is administered. The more stable an organization or an institution is – and the school is certainly one of the more stable – and the more deeply entrenched it is in the social matrix, the more difficult it becomes to make it respond to external changes. The so-called social lag is a well-known, and sometimes frustrating, phenomenon in education as an institution.

One might ask to what extent a certain lag between the development of society at large and the educational subsystem is unavoidable. Is there any reason to believe, as did the Swedish School Commission in an optimistic report which it submitted to the government in 1948, that the educational system can act 'as a propelling and progressive force in our society', a kind of optimism that was aired by many people who represented the 'new education' after World War II. There is ample reason to believe that the schools are lagging behind because of the social mechanisms involved and that the problem faced by educational planners is to reduce the lag to a minimum. Professor C. H. Beeby in his book on *Quality of Education in Developing Countries* (Harvard University Press, Cambridge, Mass., 1966) some years ago advanced a model of the growth of the primary school system as related to teacher education. I shall not describe in detail the four developmental stages that Professor Beeby distinguishes, from the first one to the fourth called 'stage of meaning'. During the first stage, called the 'dame school', teaching is relatively unorganized and to a large extent a play with meaningless symbols, with memorization being the important thing. The next stage is characterized by rigid organization and methods, with 'the one best way'. Examinations and inspection are heavily stressed and discipline is strict. Memorization has become even more important. The third stage is that of transition. The fourth one, finally, is characterized by emphasis on meaning and understanding, problem solving and pupil activity. Discipline is more relaxed and positive. More stress is put on the emotional life of the children. The main thesis that Professor Beeby advances is that, by and large, we cannot have a much better educational system than the societal context in which it is operating. Attempts that have been made in developing countries to introduce advanced educational technology have often failed because such approaches require not only a certain level of competence in the teachers but also a certain sociocultural level in the parents to make the children responsive to the particular methods of instruction.

It would take me too far to pursue this problem further. I have however, taken it up because I think that there is much evidence in support of the contention that education cannot serve as a substitute for social and economic reforms. The latter must to a large extent precede educational change. I think that we ought to be aware of the fact that we cannot change the basic pattern of a society or bring about an enhanced standard of living just by injecting into it more and better education. Education seems to have its proper place in an inherent sequence of cultural and social transformations. Sweden provides a case in point of how educational change has in the first place to be conceived within the framework of national priorities. An American, Professor Rolland Paulston, recently conducted a study of the historical background of the Swedish school reforms, particularly those pertaining to school structure. The basic issue in the Swedish reform debate since the end of the nineteenth century has been the parallelism or duality of the system, which meant that rather early some children, as a rule from well-to-do homes, transferred from the early grades in the primary school to the secondary, university-preparing academic school. The Social Democratic party early declared its allegiance to a comprehensive system which covered the entire compulsory school period. The attempts to establish a six-year basic school for all children during the 1920s failed because sufficient political backing in the parliament could not be secured. Even within the Social Democratic party a fraction of teachers were against the reform which was said to 'lower standards' in the secondary school. The legislation passed by the Swedish *Riksdag* in 1927 was a compromise between the dualistic and comprehensive camp in so far as a 'double transfer' from primary to academic secondary education was granted. When the Social Democrats came into political power at the beginning of the 1930s they took, for a long period, only a marginal interest in reforming education. Social and economic reforms aiming at full employment and social security were in the forefront. The unemployment among highly educated people led many radicals to a tacit acceptance of the dualistic or élitist system, provided that more lower class students could be granted access to higher levels of education. During the so-called 'harvest time' after 1945 the Social Democrats again brought the reform of education into focus and it became one of the major political targets. The country embarked on twenty-five years of educational change which was successively enacted by an almost unanimous parliament. The lesson to be learned from the Swedish experiences is among other things that legislation and implementation of the welfare state to a large extent has to precede commitments to educational change. First come full employment and decent standards of living and then education.

Resistance to change

I pointed out that educational reforms, irrespective of whether they aim to bring the educational system in line with social and cultural transformations, are often running against well-established and deeply entrenched institutional forces. In a society where education increasingly tends to become the democratic substitute for inherited wealth and privileged background and where demands for equality of opportunity become vociferous, change tends to be regarded as a threat to the prerogatives of the establishment and is therefore strongly resisted. These forces are primarily operating at the political level. But resistance to change within the educational system itself can be even stronger because of the more pronounced vested interests in the *status quo* that the representatives of the system have. In 1958, when about one-quarter of the school districts in Sweden had introduced the nine-year comprehensive school on a trial basis, the Swedish Radio Corporation sponsored a public opinion poll on the changing school situation. The poll showed that between one-half and two-thirds of the public preferred the comprehensive system, about one-quarter was against it and the rest were undecided. Thus at a period when the overwhelming majority of the secondary school teachers, who were accustomed to an élitist system with pronounced selective features, were rejecting the blueprint for the educational system which was laid down in the 1950 Education Act, the majority of the electorate was in favour of it. In the *Riksdag* the backing of the reform was even more overwhelming. No votes had to be taken on major points in the education bills.

The basic issue on which controversy focused was whether and to what extent the learned, academic, élitist, high-prestige, university-preparing secondary school should be replaced by a unitary school to which all the children living in a certain catchment area should be assigned. Admission to the élitist secondary school was competitive and based on standardized marks obtained in the primary school. A considerable portion of those who were selected for the secondary school later either repeated one or more grades or dropped out. Thus the teachers were instrumental in deciding the fate of the students and in fact served as a kind of gatekeeper to the establishment. Both selection for the academic schools and grade-repeating occurring during the course of study were related to student social background.

Even in a country with a social and ethnic homogeneity such as Sweden's a changeover from a dualistic and selective to a comprehensive and unitary system is quite an educational revolution. Teachers who were used to teaching a select group of students, rather homogeneous in ability and even more so in social background, were suddenly faced with the task of teaching a group representing a much wider range with regard to scholastic ability, motivation and home background. They had been trained for and were used to a system where a considerable attrition in terms of grade-repeating and drop-out took place, but were now compelled to take care of all the students and could not get rid of those who were considered unsuitable for academic exercises. Several euphemistic terms were invented for the non-academic students during the changeover period. They were labelled the 'non-theoretical' as opposed to the 'theoretical'. A more picturesque label was 'book-tired', which expressed lack of interest in academic pursuits.

The 1950 Education Act envisaged new teacher training institutions which were supposed to spread the germs of educational reform to new generations of teachers. The reform called for a new conception of the role of the teacher. Among other things, the reshaping implied a more individualized approach in teaching which would call for more work *with* the children than work *on* them or *for* them.

In 1960, four years after the first new school of education had been put into operation, the 1957 Governmental School Commission sponsored a survey comprising all teacher candidates in all types of training institutions a few weeks before graduation. The survey had two major aims:

(1) To find out how informed the young teachers were about the school reform, its aims, its organizational set-up, the new instructional methods and their implications for the role of the teachers.
(2) To assess their attitudes toward the same aspects of the reform as were considered under point 1.

Those who were trained at the new school of education were significantly better informed than those who had been trained at the traditional institutions. The prospective middle grade teachers were more favourable to the reform than were the prospective upper grade teachers. For instance, twice as many of the upper grade teachers endorsed the statement that a comprehensive system by and large best suits students who do not intend to prepare for university and are heading for vocational programmes. The attitudes towards the reform were more favourable among the trainees at the school of education. One could of course expect that teachers whose role was more deeply affected by the reform would take a less favourable attitude than those whose role was less affected. The drastic changes in the organizational structure occurred at the upper grades and caused serious concern among secondary school teachers.

It could also be hypothesized that information about and attitude towards the school reform were positively correlated, and more so for teachers at the upper grades. The correlation between information and attitude scores was 0·24 for middle grade and 0·46 for upper grade teachers. The correlation was higher for those whose working conditions were more profoundly affected by the reform and who therefore could be expected to be more strongly emotionally involved for or against a change.

What lessons could be learned from these findings and from the experiences at large in the educational scene in Sweden during the 1950s up to the legislation about the comprehensive school in 1962 and the *gymnasium* (the academic upper secondary school) in 1964? In the first place it should be emphasized that the structural change, the abolition of 'differentiation', was the main issue and therefore was in the focus of interest until legislation put an end to the controversy. The so-called 'inner reform', the adaptation of the instructional methods to the goals of the schools, had just begun. Secondly, a reform of teacher training should be concomitant with reforms of structure and curriculum because of the extremely extended time lag between teacher preparation and the full stocktaking in the classroom. It is a matter of decades even if, as has been the case in Sweden, an intensive in-service training is put into operation. Thirdly, efforts to inform can yield a substantial pay-off in terms of less defensive attitudes toward change.

Reforms of school structure, timetables, etc. can nominally and superficially be accomplished by legislation and implemented by administrative decrees. The classroom effects of curriculum prescriptions, however, might be minimal. Most studies of teachers' classroom behaviour indicate that the average teacher of the 1960s on both sides of the Atlantic seems to behave in very much the same way as he did twenty or forty years ago. Travers analysed the verbal behaviour of eighty-three American teachers and found that about one-quarter of the behaviour pertained to classroom administration, another quarter to assigning tasks and one-third to instruction in which putting questions to the students was most prevalent. Similar findings are reported by Tausch in Germany and Stukát and Engström in Sweden. The main approach is the 'frontal' one: the teacher turns to the entire class. He is controlling and teaching in the first place a group and not individual students.

Causes of resistance to change

One is certainly justified in asking why time-honoured practices prevail in spite of the fact that they are running contrary to basic notions of how children develop and learn. Why do instructional approaches frequently violate accepted psychological principles and findings of learning and differential psychology taught in the basic courses in general and/or educational psychology? For instance, grouping practices, for which there is no scientific support, are widely employed.

We can advance at least two major explanations which account for the sometimes frustrating experience that researchers repeatedly have, namely that their findings, even those which are highly conclusive, have little, if any, impact upon what is happening in the classroom.

Educational practices *are* indeed deeply entrenched, because they have prevailed for decades, not to say centuries. Even minor changes, for instance in the emphasis on different topics in teaching a given subject, might take quite a time. The teaching role is tied to heavy anchors. When we conducted a survey of the teaching of the mother tongue in the upper section of the primary school at the end of the 1950s, we concluded that the curriculum that had been issued by the government in 1919 had finally been universally implemented!

Second, and equally important, is the explanation that the major strategy in bringing about change and innovation has been to do things *to*, or at best *for*, the

teachers and not *with* them. The point, which I am going
to elaborate later in this chapter, is that the framework
within which innovative actions so far have been taken
ought to be thoroughly reshaped. I shall therefore spend
the major portion of what remains of this presentation on
describing a framework within which I think that a flexible
attitude could develop. The problem we continuously face
as educators and researchers with innovative intentions is
that changes cannot be introduced in a piecemeal way.
Even the best practices can easily fail if they are embedded
in a traditional and static pattern. But before spelling out a
philosophy of educational innovation in modern society, I
shall for a while focus on the process of translating
research findings into adopted classroom practices. We all
know that this is a long and complicated process.

Paul Mort once stated that it takes fifty years for a new
educational principle to be generally accepted and
another fifty years for it to permeate instruction, at a time
when it has already become obsolete. Actual studies
pertaining to the use, for instance, of new curricula, team
teaching and instructional material provide us, however,
with the encouraging findings that innovation does not
proceed so slowly.

In the first of the more comprehensive handbooks on
educational innovation, edited by Matthew Miles in 1964,
the editor makes a distinction between two types of
innovative strategies. (1) The change may be initiated by
the target system itself (the school system to be changed),
or (2) by other systems in the environment of the target
system. This might be a good distinction on the American
scene. But in highly centralized systems such as exist in
many European countries, change is often not only
initiated by central government but also implemented by its
administrative decrees.

From basic research to general adoption

The translation of change from the isolated university setting to the schools in the field is a four-step operation. (1) Problems are subjected to scientific study whereby new knowledge is advanced. (2) Research findings are transformed into innovative practice, including testing and evaluation in real school settings. (3) Established practices are diffused to a considerable number of schools or school systems. (4) Adoption takes place. There are certain actions associated with each stage of this procedure.

Concepts derived from basic research findings would have to be subjected to feasibility research under 'optimal' school conditions, for instance in a university laboratory school with a highly competent and research-minded teaching staff which is in continuous touch with the researchers.

A small group of 'ordinary' schools will have to be selected in order to serve as a testing ground, with the aim of finding out whether the new concepts or set-ups really work under normal classroom conditions. This requires a certain amount of initial interest and willingness to co-operate on the part of these schools and on the other hand an openness and willingness to provide assistance on the part of the research centre. Thus certain deviations within reasonable limits from general school practices are expected from the participating schools or school systems. The project centre will have to provide consultants and conduct seminars and conferences and must not forget to give teachers who want to conduct graduate work in connection with the project opportunity to do so.

The third step, the diffusion of the new set of practices, is to put them into practice in a rather large group of demonstration schools spread all over the country or the region. These schools will then serve as the final bridge between research and actual school practice at the grassroots level. The contact with the research centre is somewhat more attenuated than during the former step but at least some selected teachers will have to be brought to summer institutes or conferences. The procedure which I have briefly sketched has for instance been employed by the Institute for the Development of Educational Activities (IDEA) which is working closely with the school of education at the University of California, Los Angeles. But similar strategies in trying to achieve innovations have been tried elsewhere, for instance at the state experimental school at Linköping in Sweden.

Another frame of reference for innovative actions

There is, as indicated above, a serious problem of frame of reference involved here. So far, at least in Europe, the conception of innovation held by many state officials, top administrators and unfortunately even by researchers has been rather authoritarian. If change is contemplated in a centralized system, a national committee of policymakers is appointed. They could be assisted by top experts who are also brooding in splendid seclusion. When changes in curriculum are contemplated, the central government appoints a group of experts at the national level. They are supposed to dream up the new ideas and concepts, eventually subject them to some testing by inviting criticism from selected educators and then tell the teachers 'how it all ought to be done'. We always meet the same model: more or less rigidly conceived plans are advanced and expected to be not only put into practice but also accepted by the teachers who carry the daily burden and toil.

But one need not be too sophisticated about how social systems change or resist change in order to understand that we cannot with reasonable success bring about change only by actions taken from above, by doing things *to* or *for* the system. If we want to achieve social (including educational) change we are entitled to enter the system and to try strategies whereby we seek to change the system from *within*. The basic problem is thereby to make the system susceptible to change, to establish a climate which reacts positively to change. The psychological task is to make explicit changes or innovations that the system *wants*. We are certainly all familiar with the classical experiment which Kurt Lewin and his associates conducted during World War II as part of an attempt by the authorities to change consumer habits among American housewives. Sheer propaganda and intensive lecturing did not work. But once the wives were invited to small group meetings, where they had an opportunity to discuss the problems with the experts and could even decide what they thought was good, considerable change occurred. Change was brought about by employing simple democratic procedure. The experts who over the years have told the teachers 'how things ought to be done' have as a rule been protected from all the frustrating paraphernalia and toil involved in the proposed changes. Those of us who are experts seem to have the somewhat naïve notion that our great ideas by some kind of inner dynamics will materialize in perfect classroom practices. The resistance we have experienced has often been explained away as procrastinating manœuvres by reactionary teachers who lack the right kind of forward looking attitude and creative imagination. We have seldom tried to get behind the unwillingness where we meet fear of the new and untried and preference for the established and time-honoured.

How then could a commitment to new practices be achieved in the individual teacher? The basic approach has already been pointed out. We must convey to the teacher in the field the idea that the experts are working with him. If we want the teacher to change basic instructional practices we should not begin by telling him that what he has so far been doing is wrong, but by helping him to discover the consequences and outcomes of his practices and thus help him to discover what is wrong. What are, for instance, the consequences of one-sided 'frontal' instruction or class teaching? What is required could, to use a new expression, be called sensitivity training. The teacher could thereby get a more detached and critical attitude toward his own practices instead of withdrawing behind defensive barriers which protect him from the serious threats of the experts. Almost 40 per cent of the primary school teachers in the city of Stockholm in a survey conducted in 1955 maintained that the advice given by psychologists and other experts in the mass media had worsened instead of improved their task as educators.

Needless to say, innovative and creative change has to be introduced by voluntary action and not by expert preaching or governmental decrees, irrespective of whether the system is centralized or not. Much of the resistance to change stems from the approach whereby the experts or the administrators tell the teachers that they have so far been wrong and that 'we', the experts, researchers or administrators are right, and that they, the teachers, should therefore follow our advice.

Why should we not try to build into our innovative strategies procedures which are strongly supported by findings from our own research? We need among other things proper positive reinforcement agents which will reward innovative behaviour. So far innovative behaviour has often been negatively reinforced. The teachers who try new practices have been punished by an increased work load and disapproval on the part of their colleagues. Even the most ardent initial enthusiasm has often been extinguished under such pressures. Far from encouraging innovation, the educational system in various ways reinforces static attitudes and practices. I need not spell out the major forces which tend to keep the system in equilibrium. Learning is supposed to occur only when the teacher does something to the children. Work is regulated by a fixed timetable. The learning tasks are chopped up into standard assignments. Extra assignments are often given as punishments. Administrative procedures inside and outside the classroom are authoritarian.

The core of the matter, then, is to help the teachers to organize the system in such a way as to reinforce innovative attitudes, creative participation and willingness to subject time-honoured practices to critical scrutiny. We need to subject the reinforcers which affect teaching behaviour to scrupulous analysis. What kind of teaching behaviour do we praise or support and what behaviour do we blame or discourage?

The simple conclusion drawn from what has so far been said is that the problem of introducing educational innovations has to be tackled mainly at the local level. We would have to work *with* the teachers, try to teach them to think creatively and thus innovatively. The implication of this is among other things that the administrative apparatus should be geared to support an innovative climate. A rigid and power-seeking bureaucracy easily develops into a cement cover that bars innovative efforts instead of providing the service needed to support the teachers in the field.

Educational innovations certainly do not come about automatically. They have to be invented, planned, initiated and implemented in a way that will make educational practices more adequately geared to the changing objectives of instruction and make them more consistent with the changing standards of instruction. A major problem is then: to what extent should these changes occur by arrangements taken within the hierarchy of public office or how much should they depend on actions taken by private groups and enterprises. The heart of the matter is how the aims of innovation are most easily to be achieved and how a sufficient degree of flexibility is to be built into the innovative process. In countries with strongly centralized national systems, change is put into motion from the national centre through the channels of bureaucracy. I can see no possibility of relying on private initiative when changing organizational structure, financing or administrative procedures. The changes in school structure in most European countries provide cases in point. Such types of innovation must be backed by legal force and administrative decrees which follow on legislation passed by the national parliament. But when it comes to changes in methods of instruction, no law forces or decree in the world can secure a more adequate instruction with regard to content and method. No central or local inspector will have any effective impact. Real influence at the grassroots level would have to depend on voluntary participation. No formal authority can impose co-operation.

A bureaucracy can achieve substantial changes in the organizational framework of an educational system, but is, by its very nature, alien to creative changes pertaining to learning itself. Innovation of this type cannot occur within a bureaucratic setting, where there is accountability up the line and supervision by those who occupy a position higher up, where the individuals at the bottom are referred to the top for decisions and where there is explication, formalization and uniform application of standards of work. But the introduction of new ways of learning in the classroom requires lateral instead of vertical delegation, voluntary instead of imposed actions. Co-operation and general agreement will work instead of close supervision.

I think that an important lesson can in this respect be learned from the work carried out by the Physical Science Study Committee (PSSC) in the United States and the co-operation that emerged between this and other private groups on the one side and public agencies on the other. Briefly, what happened when the physics curriculum was upgraded was the concerted action of a governmental agency and a non profit making research corporation which marvellously cut across the power structure of both the public agencies and the national organizations. The National Science Foundation, a semi-federal agency, subsidized a private group which took the initiative to curriculum construction that required funds of a size that no private publisher could venture. The PSSC prepared the material, consisting of an impressive package of tests, manuals, films, laboratory material, etc., and offered it to the textbook industry. Within a few years the material had been adopted to the extent that it was used by half the high school students who took physics. The Yale sociologist Burton Clark, who has studied how patterns of innovation worked in this case, thinks that 'it is doubtful if a national ministry with full authority over a national curriculum could have changed the study of physics more in the same period'.

My point is that the central or governmental agencies should financially support construction of, for instance, instructional packages at schools of education, within publishing houses and within autonomous educational groups without bureaucratic formalism. This by no means excludes a certain 'steering' on the part of the sponsor. The framework is set by the ministry by the way it is spending its funds. It seems to me that interesting case studies of alliances between governmental agencies, universities, educational organizations, committees and publishing houses could be carried out in several countries. The aim of such studies would be to elucidate how innovations are brought about and how disseminations of them take place outside the channels of formal bureaucracy but nevertheless influence its work.

The thesis advanced about grassroots changes is based

on an optimistic conception of the human being. But the educational enterprise has long enough been run according to a motivational theory which says that students learn because they want to avoid unpleasant consequences. This is one of all the conceptions that run contrary to what psychology says about how human beings react. My belief is that there are energies and creative elements *within* the individual that are essential and should be brought to bear on the innovative process. An open and continuous dialogue between the teacher, the student and the expert can elicit these energies.

Two decades of educational research in Sweden

The 1950s: a setting up period for educational research

Educational research in Sweden was greatly spurred by the establishment of the State Institute of Educational Psychology in 1944 and the Council for Social Science Research in 1948, as well as by the orders for special studies which came from the various governmental commissions of inquiry into the educational system. However, these events did not suffice to give educational research, especially that with bearings on school education, its own profile. Towards that end the subject had to be represented by separate university disciplines. It may therefore be in order to portray its institutional framework as it appeared at the beginning of the 1960s. An inventory of events will disclose that the most important of them took place during the decade after 1948.

A start was made by splitting up the combined chairs in psychology and education which existed at the universities up to that time: thus Uppsala was given a separate chair of education in 1948, Stockholm in 1953, Lund in 1955 and Göteborg in 1956. In its policy report in 1948 the 1946 School Commission proposed that the first school of education – the one in Stockholm – which was later approved by the 1954 *Riksdag* be provided with a chair of educational research. It was supposed to tie in closely with the trial programme for the new comprehensive school authorized by the *Riksdag* in 1950. In other words, concentration would be on those practical problems of education that were brought to the fore by the school reform. Co-operation was to be established with teachers of methods and supervisors of student teaching so that their work could be permeated by a less dogmatic and more experimental attitude to teacher training. The new institution at the Stockholm school of education, which became operational in the autumn of 1956, was almost immediately entrusted with a series of large-scale research projects that were initiated either by the 1957 Governmental School Commission or by the institution itself.

Apart from the decision in principle to establish schools of education with professorships in education, the 1950 school legislation had other consequences. A special department of school experimentation was set up at the National Board of Education (Norinder, 1957). Since the ruling contained a recommendation for 'incessant' comparisons between the 'old' and 'new' school, the board felt called upon to make studies of how the comprehensive school performed in comparison with the lower secondary academic school (*realskola*). A considerable portion of the department's resources was accordingly spent on survey research, which amounted to administering achievement and attitude tests to randomly sampled pupils in both school types. Some idea of the scope this programme took may be formed from reading the comprehensive report which the board turned over to the Governmental School Commission in 1959. This kind of research triggered off a debate, much of it highly polemical, that went on throughout the 1950s (Husén, 1962a). The main scientific benefits may be said to have consisted in making researchers more aware of the methodological problems involved in experimental design as compared to survey design, and indeed more aware of evaluation problems in education generally (Sjöstrand, 1967). As late as the mid-1950s the very concept (and even more the term) of 'evaluation' was still unfamiliar to most educational research workers in the country. Actually, it was not until 1957 that the matter came up for discussion at a conference organized by the Scandinavian committee of experts on educational research and school experimentation.

Early consideration was given to the question of starting separate laboratory or experimental schools, which would provide not only 'optimal conditions', e.g. by means of a specially selected staff of teachers, but also facilities to keep teaching under better control through scientific method. The 1950 *Riksdag* came out in principle for such schools. A special investigation was made by the Board of Education, which recommended six schools for experimental purposes. But only one state experimental school was formed, in Linköping in 1958. Since Linköping did not then have a higher institution of teacher training, the school of education in Stockholm had to provide the institutional linkage. During the ten years of its existence the Linköping school also constituted a pilot plant in the sense of offering a test ground for the methodology with whose help educational innovations could be disseminated into the field. This school came to perform a pioneering mission for those didactic studies which require continuous contact between the teachers involved and the investigators who design and evaluate the studies. It can be said that the experiences gained from the projects operated by the state experimental school partly underlie the 'action research' contemplated for the 'laboratory and demonstration' schools which as from 1968 were established at all schools of education in consequence of the 1967 legislation on teacher training.

The need for professional psychologists and recommendations for their training comprised the main terms of reference for a government commission of inquiry appointed in 1953. In its report presented in 1955 the commission also proposed establishing a special research council in the field of education and psychology. That recommendation was partly implemented in 1957, when the State Institute of Educational Psychology was dissolved and had its staff transferred to the Institute of Educational Research at the school of education in Stockholm. However, the grant-giving function remained in the form of a research council, also called the State Institute for Psychological and Educational Research. The latter operation was merged in 1959 with the Social Science and Legal Research Council into the Council for Social Science Research, and thereby became a section of that body.

Up to the late 1940s the Swedish business community showed no more than lukewarm interest in educational questions generally. But then things began to change rapidly with the founding in the late 1940s of the Industrial Council for Social and Economic Studies (SNS), which lost no time in committing itself to school problems which had particular relevance for industry and business. In connection with preparing an evaluation of the final report of the 1946 School Commission, SNS undertook to make certain studies, of which one was concerned with the talent reserve (SNS, 1950). SNS later entered as an initiating partner in the very extensive project relating to curricula for the three upper grades of basic school, which was carried out jointly with the 1957 Governmental School Commission. This project was the most demanding of resources that educational research in Sweden had ever tackled up to that time (Husén and Dahllöf, 1965).

No historical review of the emerging educational research in Sweden would be complete without mention of the personnel selection unit that was set up at the recruiting and replacement office of the Swedish armed forces; this unit among other things made it possible to collect educational data for virtually complete cohorts of 20 year olds. This permitted survey-type studies of, for example, the size of the talent reserve or the relations between school achievement and social background. In 1948 came an opportunity to identify and collect follow-up data for the male half of those 1,500 10 year olds who had been tested in 1938 and whose social background was then charted (Husén, 1969).

Directions of research

Given the rapid expansion of educational research in Sweden during the 1950s and 1960s, attempts to pinpoint dominant trends or general characteristics pose much greater difficulties than outlining the institutional framework. Up to the mid-1950s the greater part of this research was harnessed to writing theses and qualifying for degrees, and as such reflected the special interests of individual research workers or graduate departments. Inasmuch as the psychology branch of the discipline (not least because of the existence of wholly psychological institutes or laboratories) had dominated the undivided degree subject, which was called education, by far the greater part of the research pursued had to do with projects in educational psychology. A detailed picture of the research carried out at the institutions and of the scholars involved may be obtained from the five-year reviews which *Skola och Samhälle* (School and society) published in 1950, 1955 and 1960. The studies listed covered a very broad spectrum, but with no more than a small number of studies which were strictly relevant to educational practice. In the early 1950s there was a dominance of projects preoccupied with methods of differential psychology and psychometrics. In Göteborg, the Jaederholm school of thought left a legacy that featured the application of factor analysis to problems of differential psychology (Elmgren, 1952). In Uppsala, Rudolf Anderberg and his disciples developed psychological aptitude tests under contract to industry and the armed forces. In Lund, emphasis had been put on psychological sex differences and on studies of twins (Siegvald, 1944, Smith, 1949). The institute of psychology in Lund had been called upon in the early 1940s to assist in the preparation of aptitude tests for the armed forces (Husén, 1949). The focus at the University of Stockholm institute of psychology (*Skola och Samhälle*, 1950) was on studies of the *gestalt* laws governing intellectual work, studies of mental processes and experiments with the motor skills involved in penmanship — all with relevance for the classroom and all carried out in the tradition of experimental psychology laid down by David Katz. When Gösta Ekman was attached to the undivided Stockholm institute, vital research into differential psychology was introduced even there.

By comparison with the Continent, educational research in Sweden has had less of a philosophical-humanistic-historical bent. Even so, this has not been without its leading exponents, especially Wilhelm Sjöstrand at Uppsala and Sven Edlund at Lund. Both men earned their doctorates in the history of education, a field that has also been the subject of dissertations of several scholars at Uppsala. Sjöstrand has compiled a comprehensive handbook of history of education for advanced studies in this subject. A considerable part of this research has been pursued outside the universities, for example by the Swedish History of Education Society, where noteworthy achievements were especially associated with the name of Albert Wiberg, the society's executive secretary. By virtue of the dominance of educational psychology, and owing to the shortage of competent teachers, the historical and comparative segments of the discipline have been neglected in some quarters not only as fields for inquiry but also as areas of teaching. One explanation for this, it seems to me, is traceable to the 1939 Universities Commission which, when it proposed splitting up the 'old' chairs of education into chairs of psychology on the one hand and chairs of education and educational psychology on the other, envisaged the humanistic segment of the subject plus its large psychological portion being ably managed by prospective holders of the 'new' chairs. But except at Uppsala and Lund, this has not happened. In view of the far-reaching specialization that the subject has developed, not least in its behavioural science aspect, it can no longer be assumed that one person alone can represent both the empirical-experimental and humanistic branches of the discipline, and his chances of assimilating all the related research are even less.

Looking at the years from 1948 in retrospect, they stand out as pervaded by the spirit of reform in education generally and in compulsory schooling in particular. The 1946 School Commission in a report of 1952 proposed the first school of education, to which should be attached a chair that would be explicitly termed 'school research'. For reasons unknown the chair subsequently came to be called 'practical pedagogy', a title that was also affixed to these ensuing chairs: in Malmö, 1961; in Göteborg, 1964; in Umeå, 1968; and in Uppsala and Linköping in 1969. The chair in Göteborg emphasizes special education. Research projects were commissioned by the different educational commissions at the same time as research institutions were formed at the schools of education which were under the authority of the National Board of Education. As a result research geared to current school problems began to emerge as an important discipline within the educational research field.

Another fillip to educational research came from the

1946 School Commission, which called upon the
Göteborg institute of psychology to make certain studies
of the maturation process in so far as this was thought to
bear upon a solution of the so-called differentiation issue
(Elmgren, 1952). As soon as educational research gets
involved in 'policy oriented' problems, it tends willy-nilly
to be drawn into political controversy. None the less,
the commitment itself tends to generate further research
in topical problem areas – and not only because research
workers find it easier to obtain funds for such studies.
When we look at what school research has done in
Britain, an overwhelming concern since 1945 has been
with the 'eleven plus' problem, that is, with attempts to
define and operationalize the criteria that should govern
admissions to grammar school (Vernon, 1957). The greater
part of this research, considered with reference to the
inputs of psychologists, has proceeded from a more or less
tacitly accepted premise, namely that a competitive
selection of pupils shall take place at the stated age. By
contrast, the British sociologists have done studies which
largely question the basic assumptions of the system
(Halsey, 1961).

In Sweden a similar sociological approach has been
taken to the differentiation problem, also by the
educational psychologists. The follow-up by Nils-Eric
Svensson (1962) of Stockholm pupils who ended up in
different pedagogic milieus and grouping practices, as well
as Sixten Marklund's (1962) study of the relationship
between homogeneity of school class and achievement
level, sought to test time-honoured assumptions of
inherent educational superiority in the *realskola* environment
and in homogenization *as such*. These studies touched off
a discussion on the respective merits of survey design
versus experimental design, with Uppsala originating most
of the criticism (Agrell, 1953; Sjöstrand, 1961). The more
experimentally patterned study of different grouping

arrangements carried out at Växjö by the Uppsala institution should be seen in the light of this discussion. Further light on methodological issues was shed by Dahllöf (1971), who subjected both the Stockholm and Växjö studies to more detailed analyses.

The outcomes of different streaming practices are evaluated not only on the basis of cognitive criteria, as measured by conventional achievement tests, but also of affective criteria. On behalf of the 1957 Governmental School Commission, Ingvar Johannesson and David Magnusson (1960) studied the relation to schoolmates and attitudes to work in different school types and classes. Similar evaluations were made in the Växjö study (Sjöstrand, 1966). These and other investigations have extended the scope of the evaluation process. The survey project relating to experimental programmes which was carried out during the 1950s under the auspices of the National Board of Education, together with the studies that originated in the work of the Governmental School Commission, probably rank as the most massive ever undertaken in a European country in connection with an educational reform, and for that reason have aroused considerable attention abroad (Husén and Boalt, 1968).

In these circumstances it became natural for a Swedish institution of educational research to take part in the International Project for the Evaluation of Educational Achievement (IEA) that commenced in 1959 (Husén *et al.*, 1967). Another reason for participation was the experience gained in Sweden in the administration of achievement tests as part of large-scale survey investigations. As a means of equalizing school marks, these tests have been taken by virtually all pupils in certain grades since the mid-1940s. At first these tests had exclusively aimed at standardizing marks, but that has now been relegated to secondary importance in the lower and middle departments of the basic school. They are now increasingly used by the teacher to evaluate his own instruction. Access to data from standard tests administered to whole grades has permitted a great deal of research that could not possibly have been managed otherwise. In 1960 a subcommittee of the Council for Social Science Research proposed that the Central Bureau of Statistics collect, at intervals of five years, a body of individual statistics which would cover standard test data, intelligence test data, social data etc. for a national random sample of one school grade. The proposal was adopted, and by now a data bank has been established which lends itself to longitudinal studies of nationally representative groups. Here it can be mentioned that Kjell Härnqvist (1966, 1968), who was instrumental in setting up the individual statistics, has enlisted the assistance of pupils to gauge the impact of educational reforms on willingness to go in for higher studies. Indeed, longitudinal data permit investigations — of for instance the effect of schooling — that are otherwise quite impracticable or that leave much to be desired if performed with cross-sectional data. Besides, Sweden has a system for registering population where the research worker need not run the risk of losing data even in cases where his study spans a very long period. The 1,500 10 year olds studied in 1938 have been followed by me and my associates up to now (Husén, 1969) ; our main purpose here was to appraise the predictive value of 1938 data for educational and vocational careers, as well as for social adjustment in general.

The curriculum research project mentioned above was initiated by the 1957 Governmental School Commission and SNS in the late 1950s, with the starting emphasis put on the course content of five subjects taught in the basic school — mathematics, mother tongue, civics, physics and chemistry. This project set itself the sweeping task of determining the relevance of subject matter for different 'user groups', whether these consisted of the forwarding schools, the business community or the pupils themselves. A similar project was sponsored by the 1960 Commission of Inquiry into the pre-university school (*gymnasium*) and strongly influenced its curriculum development (Dahllöf, 1963). This research area has since been further developed, for instance by Dahllöf (1971), who designed a model for 'comparative goal and process analyses'. The overriding concern here is with those process variables that operate in the actual classroom, such as methods and instruction time, and their relation to the outcomes of teaching. Intertwined with this research there has also evolved an educational technology, which will be dealt with below.

It will have emerged from the foregoing that educational research in Sweden is closely allied to the behavioural sciences. The liaison with psychology has been especially intimate for historical reasons. Most of the leading researchers learned their methodology under the aegis of psychology. One example is Karl Gustaf Stukát (1966), who has published the first Swedish manual on educational research methodology. However, the same reasons account in part for the close contact with sociology. The first Swedish chair in sociology was instituted at the University of Uppsala in 1948. Its incumbent, Torgny Segerstedt, has devoted much of his labour to building up a theoretical framework for research into educational sociology. Many of the junior researchers who later became professors or joined the new sociological institutions had received their basic behavioural science training in the days before education was formally separated from psychology. I see this as the essential explanation not only for the fact that Swedish behavioural scientists more or less talk the same language, but also for their having grappled with similar problems to such a great extent. The consequence has been that educational sociology has become a common meeting ground for many of them. It is striking to see how many researchers, who are formally classified as psychologists, pedagogues or sociologists, have carried out or taken part in major survey studies intended to elucidate important educational problems. Several examples of this will be given below.

During the latter part of the 1940s military recruitment data were used to make the first large-scale investigations into the size of the so-called reserve of talent. They gave rise to a methodological debate which engaged social scientists from different disciplines. A considerably improved methodology developed by Ekman (1951) entered into the talent reserve study that was sponsored by the 1955 Universities Commission (Härnqvist, 1961), and that too touched off a lively debate. It is interesting to advert here to a similar study made by Dael Wolfle (1954) in the mid-1950s, which employed methods that were cruder than the ones concurrently used in Sweden. The extent of the research and its attendant debate can be measured by the bibliography that appended an overview of the field in the 1962 *Yearbook of Education* (Husén, 1962; cf. Husén, 1972).

The findings of Sweden's first major project in educational sociology were presented by Gunnar Boalt (1947), who had followed up a whole fourth grade in Stockholm for ten years. His object was to analyse the significance of social background for school career and scholastic achievement. Several years later came the presentation of a ten-year follow-up of male pupils in grade 3 in Malmö, who had been tested when they registered for military service (Husén, 1951). This study made it possible to take new approaches to gauge the relative weight of social background for success in school. In connection with the study of streaming in Stockholm undertaken by the 1957 Governmental School Commission, where a random sample of pupils was followed from grade 4 to 9, it was also possible to evaluate the role of social background for admissions to and rejections from the *realskola*, as well as for non-promotions and failures in that school. The findings presumably determined to a great degree the stand taken by the committee on grouping in the three upper grades of basic school (Svensson, 1962).

At this juncture fitting mention can also be made of some relatively new research projects, mainly of the survey type, especially Project Youth in Göteborg (Andersson, 1969) and the Örebro project (Magnusson *et al.*, 1966). Both these projects are of the kind that require large-scale teamwork. Project Youth generally aims to study youth values and to plumb the attitudes to education and vocational choice of pupils enrolled in grades 8 and 9 of basic school, while the Örebro project is mainly concerned with the adjustment mechanisms of school youth. In 1960 the Council for Social Science Research provided for a separate research fellowship at the school of education in Stockholm to look into the special problems of adjustment that were expected to arise when compulsory schooling would apply to virtually all youngsters up to the age of sixteen. The appointment was filled by Ingvar Johannesson (1966), who kept it until 1967. He has mainly focused on the attitudes to school and schoolmates of pupils in grades 7–9.

In the border area between social psychology and the psychology of personality, a considerable body of sociometric research has evolved at Lund University, and afterwards at the school of education in Malmö (Bjerstedt, 1956). Among fundamental method studies, mention can be made of the one performed by Åke Bjerstedt (1963), who has also done a sociopsychological study of international children's villages in Sweden.

The important investigative work carried out during the first half of the 1960s by the 1960 Governmental Committee on teacher training represented some pioneering research achievements (Marklund, 1968). For example, the committee has mapped out the instruction given in a number of university subjects (Elgqvist, 1965) and produced monographs dealing with the study of education as a discipline in teacher training. Here again the work of official committees has provided an incentive for significant educational research.

Other conspicuous features of the Swedish research landscape are the extensive projects concerned with reading and spelling (Norinder, 1946 ; Husén, 1951 ; Edfeldt, 1959 ; Malmquist, 1962 ; Wallin, 1968). Studies of reading have played a prominent role in the research programme launched by Eve Malmquist (1958), the director of research at the first state experimental school.

Lastly, studies with important educational implications have been carried out by such bodies as the Swedish Council for Personnel Administration, for example Ejnar Neymark's (1961) research into selective migration, and the Institute of Applied Psychology at the University of Stockholm, for example studies of the prediction value of tests and marks for entry into limited-enrolment faculties at universities and colleges.

The situation at the end of the 1960s

With educational research in Sweden caught up in a dynamic growth process boosted by rapid increase in funds until the end of the 1960s, we do not have sufficient perspective to permit a description of the present state of the art. None the less, an attempt must be made to extrapolate tendencies that have stood out since the beginning of the 1960s.

To begin with, a few more important ingredients should be added to the institutional picture, since they have come to bear crucially on the resources available to research at the end of the decade. The funds that the Council for Social Science Research is able to allot to psychological-pedagogical research have increased substantially. Two

new sources of grants have arrived on the scene, namely
the Bank of Sweden Tercentenary Fund and the special
bureau (L3) for educational R and D in the school sector
set up by the National Board of Education in 1962. A
similar bureau was established in 1969 at the Office of the
Chancellor of the Universities. The Tercentenary Fund has
awarded very large grants to extensive sociological-
educational projects of the type COMPASS (comparative
analyses of processes and goals) (Dahllöf, 1967),
Metropolit (a follow-up of young people in Scandinavian
capitals) and IEA (both the international and national
portions thereof) (Husén *et al.*, 1967). The course of
events reflects the expectations which government
authorities put into educational research concerning
desirable or necessary innovations within the educational
research concerning desirable or necessary innovations
within the educational system. The legislation on the
basic school (1962) and on upper secondary education
(1964) implied that questions of school structure were no
longer in the forefront. Instead, so we were told, the
overriding task would be to renew the school's internal
work, methods of instruction and teaching aids – with
research serving as one of the beacons. However, the
school reforms have come to place enormous demands on
the national exchequer. Over a span of somewhat more
than one decade, expenditures per pupil at constant prices
have nearly doubled. That plus the shortage of teachers,
which has bottlenecked the reform programme throughout
the 1960s, has engendered demands for rationalizations or
more efficient methods of operation. The budget request
submitted by the Board of Education for the 1968–9
fiscal year argued efficiency criteria on almost every page.
Hence the central issue has come to be : how does one
go about achieving a renewal of the school's work that
conforms with the new curricula, *at the same time* as the
school's 'production forms' are rationalized to get more out

of every pupil for each krona invested than is now the case. Since the biggest cost item consists of teacher salaries, the main focus has naturally been on finding new methods to permit better economic management of the nation's educational manpower (Husén, 1971).

Bureau L3 functions for the most part as a 'monitoring' agency for the school research that has been going on at the country's pedagogical institutes since the early 1960s. Some are subordinated to the Board of Education since they are incorporated with schools of education. The bureau may either receive project proposals from interested individual senior research workers at an institution or itself approach an institution where a favourable reception can be counted on and which will be called upon to submit project proposals. As a rule, this is a matter of negotiations on a more informal level before a more official request goes out in either direction.

The projects backed by bureau L3 may be schematically grouped in three categories. First of all, there are comprehensive material-methods projects which aim at producing prototypes for a teaching aids system, either with reference to a specified school department or a specified grade within a given subject field. Among the more or less completed projects in this category, mention may be made of individualized instruction in mathematics (IMU), instruction methods in English (UME) and teaching material for instruction in religion (UMRe) (Ahlström, 1967). The purpose of these projects has been to create integrated systems of teaching aids which can be expected to effect changes in the school's working situation that cannot be attained by curricular directives or recommendations alone. The key factor in this picture is to have centralized commitment to the preparation of methods, materials and organization which are necessary prerequisites for individualized instruction. The point is raised because it may be doubted whether projects of this type have any place at all in educational research institutions, considering that these by definition have to be mainly concerned with problems of basic or conclusion oriented research and as such should therefore not get over-involved in development work, e.g., the straightforward production of materials (Husén, 1968a). A similar question has been put in respect of the research and development centres located at some ten American universities. It can be answered by saying that basic research and applied research tend to fertilize one another when carried on at the same institution, provided that an appropriate balance can be maintained between them. Furthermore, work on applied projects can impart urgency to problems of basic research that would otherwise not have come up for consideration. The most pressing problem for these institutions until the beginning of the 1970s has been the shortage of qualified researchers. The teacher training reform, not to mention the surge of enrolments in the schools of education, has generated a greatly increased need for lecturers in education. For this reason, the Board of Education has lent different kinds of support to projects which seek to train educational research workers.

In addition to the R and D connected with the development of teaching aid systems, a more systematic methodology has been enlisted to tackle the problem of teacher training. Towards this end projects which employ closed-circuit television have commenced in Stockholm, Göteborg and Malmö. The Göteborg school of education has developed a special method of observing teacher behaviour by means of closed-circuit TV (Stukát and Engström, 1968). The need to evaluate the long-term effects of the new teacher training programme triggered off the KUL project (qualitative evaluation of teacher training).

Thinking in terms of educational technology and the kind of research that goes with it accounts for the training of educational technologists that has started at the

University of Göteborg. This programme must be seen as an attempt to meet the need for educators who have learned to think in 'material-methods' terms on the basis of fundamental schooling in the behavioural sciences. One of the great problems – as yet largely unsolved – for research affiliated with the schools of education is the difficulty of getting methods instructors and student-teaching supervisors to combine research with teaching. In the days when the 1946 School Commission was making its inquiries, it envisaged in its report on teacher training that student teachers would be able to pursue graduate studies in subject methodology at schools of education. Apart from the fact that the proposal to this effect was rejected by the universities, nor for that matter was it taken up in the government bill which provided for the first school of education, the efforts to bring about methods research failed largely because of the difficulties of applying behavioural-science thought to the didactic field. The latter often takes on the character of recipes that are not always rationally founded or supported by research findings. The project groups which combine the researching talents of a behavioural scientist with those of a qualified teacher of didactics and one or more assistants have so far proved to be the most useful solution to the dilemma herein indicated. Under this arrangement most of the didactic research has come to be pursued at the institutes of education.

Swedish behavioural research at the outset of the 1950s, irrespective of whether it carried an educational or psychological label, was essentially marketed as social engineering, which more or less amounted to telling people what they were good for. It could help to predict who was going to be able to cope with higher education or it could demonstrate aptitude for certain occupations. Expectations of this kind were for instance put by the National Board of Education during the 1940s in the projected State Institute of Educational Research that was supposed to grapple with problems bearing upon the school system. Psychological tests were to be designed that would 'differentiate' pupils and ascertain their 'aptitudes and traits' in connection with vocational guidance. As things turned out, such tasks in so far as they related to pupils in the compulsory school were relegated to the background to the same extent that organizational differentiation was deferred until after the end of basic schooling (Husén and Boalt, 1968). At that point, however, the problem crops up again with undiminished force – albeit not with the same once-and-for-all finality for the individual as when it was decided at the age of eleven who should not enter the state secondary grammar school.

The question of guiding the pupils at upper secondary level, where the *Riksdag* has decided to offer some twenty programmes, has made it imperative to provide policymakers with data for their decisions. Psychometrics, whose main research contribution to education in Sweden so far has consisted of designing aptitude tests and standard achievement tests, has been called upon to explore the predictive value – for upper secondary studies – of information about pupils in the upper department of basic school. Since the mid-1960s Sten Henrysson (1967), a leading expert in the field, has been doing a large-scale follow-up of all pupils in Västmanland province who moved up from basic school to some kind of secondary education. The Västmanland (VLM) study, which is longitudinal in character, has in recent years been pursued further by Bengt Olov Ljung (1970) and associates at the Stockholm school of education. Studies of this character also have relevance to the assessment of qualifications that must be made in a society which on the one hand seeks to modify or even remove formal requirements for admission to post-secondary education, yet on the other hand has so many applicants for admission to most faculties that some kind of selection must take place. The question that must then be asked is: what formal requirements should be asked of the applicants, and which methods of testing scholastic ability can be regarded as the most adequate technically?

A major spur to strict thinking in terms of educational technology has been the advent of programmed instruction aids. Educational technology is in no way tied to apparatus or mechanical devices of any kind. Its central animus is the quest to analyse carefully and to express in behavioural terms the objectives of learning, and in so doing to organize occasions for learning which optimize the potential for individualization. Research into programmed learning has been pursued in different parts of Sweden. In Göteborg a task force was busily engaged during the early 1960s. In Malmö the school of education has done significant work on programming problems (Bjerstedt, 1965). In Uppsala, Karl Georg Ahlström (1967) has, in connection with the SMID project there, looked into different ways of presenting programmed material. Not only have his studies had great impact on basic research into learning, but Ahlström has on the whole played a leading part in modern research of this kind which has had more direct pedagogical applications.

Future perspectives

By way of conclusion, it may be in order to venture an assessment of the direction in which present tendencies in educational research are pointing. Such an assessment has already been made by a subcommittee of the Council for Social Science Research which was called upon to submit that body's report on educational research to the Swedish Government Research Advisory Board (Samhällsforskning, 1968). With the substance of this report in mind, I confine myself to bringing up certain points as follows.

In consequence of the 1967 parliamentary ruling, all courses in education that relate to the training of teachers have been sited at schools of education. The course in psychology cum theory and history of pedagogy, which once upon a time justified the existence of chairs of pedagogy at the universities, has now been abolished. What, indeed, could be more natural than to have the schools of education take that part of educational research which is called school research under their wing? That has given rise to co-ordination problems as a matter of course, since our country is certainly not so richly endowed with teaching and researching talents in the educational sphere that we can afford to have two parallel research organizations, each with its own sponsor, in most of our university towns. These co-ordination problems, together with the question of educational resources in general, have been under consideration by a Governmental Commission on research and teaching in education.

In the report handed over to the Swedish Government Research Advisory Board, we read that 'pedagogical research has nowadays also taken on important duties outside what we normally call the instruction field'. Learning has become a lifelong process, and instruction must be seen as only one sector within a system which constantly influences the individual to learn something or other. Particular reference should be made in this context to the philosophy which has evolved at the institute of education at Stockholm University, where education is defined as '. . . a system of methods for exerting influences that must be adaptable to the specific determinants in every part of society, which will require changing the norms, ideas, skills etc. of individuals acting in the system'. As thus conceived, the discipline of education is looked upon as a general science of behavioural changes. In concrete terms it signifies that research into problems of social welfare, old-age care, penology and other social therapy is considered as belonging in part to the realm of educational research.

The technological programme of research and training initiated at Göteborg University should be seen as an attempt to specify new goals for the conventional sector of pedagogical research concerned with upbringing and schooling. The advent of an institutionalized system of adult education has given impetus to research in the field of adult pedagogy. Upon the recommendation of the Adult Education Committee, a readership in adult education was established at the Stockholm school of education with emphasis put on initiating research in this field. The National Board of Education is subsidizing this post, as well as a project in adult education which got under way at Uppsala University in the mid-1960s.

At the time these lines were being written it was possible to foresee important missions for the universities in the field of academic pedagogy. Proceeding from an analysis of needs, an ad hoc committee proposed that the Office of the Chancellor of the Swedish Universities be given an agency that would most closely correspond to bureau L3 at the National Board of Education. The committee itself initiated a large number of projects dealing with 'put-throughs', examinations, etc. A bureau responsible for R and D work related to university instruction has been established.

It it perhaps symptomatic that the National Board of Education decided in 1968 to back a project which deals with the development of the school system up to the year 2000 (Husén, 1971). The authorities must constantly draw their plans with a time focus that takes in several decades. More intuitive judgements of the 'futurological' kind must be based with more systematic analyses and attempted projections that are not too unimaginative. The prospects for coping with the enrolment and knowledge explosions in the educational sector, and not only in the technical sense, will greatly depend on the provision that is made for new approaches to the purposes of formal education in a society which will have to be emancipated from inadequate institutional forms, and where the individual will have to be more flexible than ever before.

As is evident from this survey account of Swedish educational research in the post-war period, the scholars have abandoned their academic ivory towers in increasing numbers, not a little enticed by the enormous resources (by earlier standards, at least) which government committees and authorities can put at their disposal. This new situation brings up two important questions. What can scholars do as research workers to help policymakers handle – I do not say 'solve' – their problems better? What problems of integrity will arise for the scholar if his work is increasingly dependent upon the grants which the authorities advance to him for specified purposes, most of them narrowly telic? I have penetrated and even tried to answer these questions in a lecture which I gave in London in the autumn of 1967, at a general assembly meeting of the National Foundation for Educational Research in England (Husén, 1968a). It may therefore suffice in this context to summarize the conclusions. As I see it, the scholar has three essential duties when he contracts to do research. (1) He must help policymakers tidy up their terms of reference. For instance, he can say it makes no sense to ask what is the 'best age' for schoolchildren to take the beginning course in the first foreign language. (2) He can make available his technical know-how, the research tools he has learned how to handle, towards working upon the terms of reference once they are properly tidied up. (3) He can help policymakers interpret the findings of completed studies, well aware that policy decisions are taken not only on the basis of the evidence he may be able to furnish, but that such decisions will

ultimately be governed by political value judgements which
– sometimes – can be influenced by the perspectives that
the scholar helps to open up.

Another question must be asked, but answering it
concisely is more difficult: what relation will guarantee the
scholar's integrity vis-à-vis the client, will protect the
scholar's undogmatic and critical attitude so that he is not
tempted to become an evangelist for fear of cutting
himself off from the pecuniary manna that flows from the
client? To my mind, the essential thing is that contract
research at an institute should not take on such
dimensions as to trap the scholar in a strict timetable,
where he is under pressure to deliver 'results' at all costs.
There must be scope for the 'irresponsible' and playful
pursuit which constitutes an integral element of all
worthwhile research, a playing with data that can yield
the most unexpected results. It is especially important for
the scholar to avoid getting ensnared in research of the
kind that makes him an executive project director, with
his workday completely absorbed by administrative tasks
and where he falls easy victim to the greatest peril of all
bureaucracy: giving top priority to making sure that the
machinery operates with technical perfection, putting
aside any qualms as to what this machinery is really
supposed to do.

The future 4

The purposes of futurological studies in education |

Introductory remarks

The young people we now have in our schools will be entering the most productive, and publicly the most influential, period of their lives in twenty to thirty years, i.e. towards the end of this century. The objectives of the education that the school gives them, and the content of the instruction they are subject to, must obviously consider that it is not today's society – much less yesterday's – that these youngsters will take charge of, but rather a society which lies only a few paltry (but oh so important) decades ahead of us, when we reflect upon the process of change that has swept across this society at an accelerated rate, especially since 1945. Accordingly, contemporary educational planning must allow for the effects it is likely to have on the society – not to mention the world – that we are going to have twenty to thirty years from now. Not even that will suffice, however. Let me take the following illustration. The Swedish *Riksdag* passed legislation on a new system of teacher training in 1967, and the first crop of teachers under the new system emerged in 1969. These teachers are expected to be active professionally for an average thirty-five to forty-five years to come. They will be teaching young people whose own productive lives will run for about fifty years. This is by way of saying that the teacher training decisions taken during the 1960s will have repercussions up to the mid-twenty-first century.

The foregoing remarks should suffice to justify futurological studies in education of the type which seek to define the consequences of present-day planning and decisions for tomorrow's school. Could it be that the schools of three decades hence will bear little if any resemblance to the time-honoured type we know today? In the present century, at any rate, 'education' and 'school' have increasingly come to be regarded as synonymous concepts. In Sweden the establishment of a compulsory elementary school was accompanied by the formal abolition of the guild system, within whose institutional framework training for the handicrafts had taken place. The apprenticeship system for training in the trades continued to linger on for some time. But during the course of the past century education has increasingly come to be carried on in the institutional forms that regular schooling has established, with grades, teacher-led class instruction, tests, marks and examinations. From time immemorial, moreover, we have learned to regard education as a matter exclusively associated with the years of our youth. In other words the basic and applied knowledge and skills needed to make our way in the world are supposed to be acquired early in life. But already at the beginning of this century the free and voluntary adult education programmes sponsored by the various people's movements developed apace, and to a large extent, at least in Scandinavia, these were detached from the institutional school system. The non-formal voluntary system by means of study circles and evening classes long focused on giving a basic general education, on imparting certain skills in, for example, the native language and society-and-nature orientation that the great masses did not receive from elementary public education, which after all was rather meagre. In other words, no question of training for careers or of imparting saleable skills was involved. But during the past decade we have been witnessing, at least in Sweden, the upsurge of adult education which aims at bread-and-butter goals. Both the traditional programmes of adult education and, to some extent, the vocationally oriented system of adult education have operated outside the traditional school framework. As regards the voluntary adult education programmes, one can discern a deliberate effort to move away from the traditional forms and towards the goals they serve.

Recent developments in adult education have opened our eyes to the fact that education takes in a great deal more than mere formal schooling in the traditional sense. The young people attending school today belong to the generation that has been exposed to television from pre-school years and that will be exposed, as transmission time increases, just as much to what comes out of the magical cathode ray tube as to what comes out of a teacher at his classroom desk. A moment's reflection tells us that the school's sphere of influence has also diminished in this respect. In the society that we have been entering for some time, education is in the process of becoming a lifelong concern for the great majority of people, and thus more than a matter to which one dedicates the years of childhood and youth. In that connection the school as an institution — and under forms that are changing drastically — will answer for only certain limited educational functions.

These sketchy indications should suffice to provide a general background to my principal topic, namely the tasks and methods of futurological studies and the visions of education that may reasonably be contemplated for the coming turn of the century.

Three cardinal purposes for futurology

What are the cardinal purposes in education that can be imagined for futurology? As far as I can see, three lines of development suggest themselves.

(1) Research can be confined to identifying the future consequences of contemporary planning and policy decisions relating to school organization, construction, curricula, teaching aids and teacher training. The layout given to a new school plant implies certain definite notions as to how work will be carried on in the projected building for many decades to come. A structure full of inner bearing walls, and divided up into classrooms of a certain size, presupposes that these rooms will have a specified number of pupils – regarded as normal for so-called class instruction in today's situation – who are going to imbibe wisdom that is mainly imparted by specially trained teachers. Planning of this kind more or less rules out certain alternatives where the school's work practices are concerned, alternatives which have a common assumption that practices will vary and that pupils will become more active. In any event, such planning has the effect of making these alternatives less likely to materialize.

The example just cited illustrates how important it is to clarify the long-range implications of today's school decisions. It also illustrates a vital thesis: futurologists do not aspire – or should not aspire – to explain what is *supposed* to happen but what *can* happen. In his book *Dialog i Det Fria* (Dialogue in the open), the Swedish writer Sven Fagerberg has a section he calls 'The soothsayers', inspired by a special issue about the year 2000 that the American periodical *Daedalus* put out in the summer of 1967. This issue was given over to presenting the results of deliberations made by a committee appointed by the US National Academy of Science. Fagerberg has this to say: 'Forecasts have . . . a great importance; they compel us to analyse the here and now and to try to understand what is happening at this moment. But they can never tell us what is going to happen.' In this way investigation into the future can also help to create that future.

As long as the investigator sticks to analysing the import and consequences of contemporary planning and policy decisions, he stands on pretty solid ground and does not have to rely too much on what he sees in the crystal ball – or whatever metaphor one wishes to use to characterize the doings of futurologists. But his task immediately becomes more difficult if he takes a step further and extrapolates the statistical trends that are now observable. And he will be tackling a really formidable task if he goes yet one more step to identify those general development patterns and value trends that will dominate society a quarter century hence. I shall have something more to say about these riskier ventures presently. But first some more viewpoints about the task of making clear the nature of the ultimate commitment that follows from decisions already taken or implemented.

I assume that all parties endorse the rational principle – by paying lip service to it, if nothing else – that educational planning, as well as social planning in general, in our changeable society ought to aim at maximum flexibility, the object being to keep open as many acceptable future alternatives as possible. That is a demand which ought to be imposed on those responsible for planning physical facilities and designing school constructions. Or to put this principle the other way round, contemporary planning should rule out as few alternatives as possible. This means that the futurologist ought to study present-day policy decision-making from two angles.

First, do today's planning and political decisions harmonize with the general objectives of public policy that have been adopted *for the long run*? Second, what future alternatives have been excised by today's actions? When the Swedish authorities decided, a few decades ago, to go in radically for centralizing schools in urban areas and shutting down the majority of the small rural schools, they were motivated by the prospect of certain administrative benefits, and perhaps economic ones as well: since large-scale educational operation would be more advantageous than continuing with the little red schoolhouse, the latter ought to be closed down. However, the transportation of young people to large urban schools which followed from the closures combined with the abandonment of farms to generate a vast depopulation of the countryside. In a recent study, Dr Sixten Marklund has shown that small schools offering middle-department courses (i.e. grades 4–6) do not perform worse than the large schools, indicating that the pure educational advantages of doing away with all the many small rural schools at the lower and middle levels have been of dubious value. On top of that, the social and economic impact on sparsely populated areas has been highly negative.

Politicians are easily tempted to look for short-term solutions to current problems. Which is perhaps understandable considering that they are reminded of their mortality at fairly brief intervals, i.e. at the regularly recurring elections. Hence they readily go astray when confronted with situations where they have to choose between that which imperils their own careers in the short run and that which imperils the voters, i.e. society, in the long run.

The administrators, especially if they work in a strongly bureaucratic setting, risk (for somewhat different reasons) losing sight not only of the future but of the basic meaning of the tasks they have in hand at the moment. Current worries, the day-to-day routine, often assume overwhelming proportions, or are perceived to be so overwhelming that

no time is left for thinking in terms of the 'long pull'. Now
it happens to be the very essence of bureaucracy not only
to build empires but also to become so engrossed in the
formal and technical perfection of a present preoccupation
that questioning the real meaning of what one is doing
seldom if ever comes to mind. A brilliant, and illuminating,
document on this point is to be found in *Grisjakten* (The
pig hunt), the book written by P. C. Jersild. Secretary
Siljeberg is so absorbed with the task his boss in the
ministry has assigned to him — to exterminate all pigs in
Sweden as efficiently as possible (starting with the
experimental district of the island of Gothland) — that he
never stops to ask what purpose all this technical perfection
is really supposed to serve.

There is something else which impedes the bureaucratic–
political establishment from inquiring into the future
consequences of its present actions. During the past five
to ten years we have seen increasingly clamorous protests —
voiced not least by today's youth — against the imputed
penchant of authorities to plan and decide over the head
of the common man. It is contended, not without reason,
that an inner circle of technicians and experts, political
experts included, steamroller decisions on city planning,
roadbuilding, school construction and water impounding
which fly in the face of what growing grassroots opinion
perceives to be desirable long-range objectives. One
example, now very much the object of controversy, is the
extent to which private automobiles should be allowed to
circulate freely in downtown areas. A great deal of prestige
readily tends to hang on questions of this kind. That which
was planned a long time ago, when the conditions were
different, builds up such powerful convictions and
momentum among the bureaucrats that it rolls on with
juggernaut force. Experts and persons in authority who have
long worked on and sweated over the issues thereby feel
they have become privy to a higher insight, and not

infrequently put on a stiff and even supercilious tone towards the protestors. In other words, they 'know better'.

(2) The futurologist can try to determine certain trends expressed in numerical terms, such as school enrolments, development of costs and use of teaching aids, and then extrapolate these trends, i.e. find out in which direction the curves are pointing. This kind of peering into the future, which amounts to drawing upon demographic data to compute the need for school plants and their sizes, has become routine nowadays in both the local and central school planning that is pursued in most quarters. Yet it was not more than a few decades ago that no one in Scandinavia seemed to think it even possible to predict with great accuracy the number of children who would be starting school six or seven years after a certain cohort was born!

Even so, attempts to extrapolate trend curves can have their parlous sides. An example is the estimate of the supply of and demand for special subject teachers that was made by the 1955 Commission of Inquiry into the Swedish universities. When the commission published its special report in 1958, it went on record as saying that secondary school teachers would already be in surplus by the early 1960s, and that the surplus would grow as the decade progressed. The analyses were based on the reported number of secondary school leavers having completed a *gymnasium* programme and passed the *studentexamen*, together with the number of matriculants and degree takers at the faculties of arts and sciences up to the mid-1950s. It could be established that the number of leavers from the pre-university school had by and large increased linearly from 1940 to 1955. The assumption was that this would continue till the mid-1960s, at which point the curve would level off, since the increase could not very well be expected to go on as in the past.

Further, it was assumed that first-year enrolments in the arts and sciences faculties would not mount substantially. Lastly, the experiences gained from the pilot programme with the nine-year comprehensive school were drawn upon for that proportion of pupils in the upper department (grades 7–9) who had made so-called academic options, a proportion which was largely identifiable with the percentage of an age group who had elected to study two foreign languages. It did not take more than a few years for the actual course of events to confute all these assumptions. The curve for secondary school leavers turned out to increase not linearly but exponentially, i.e. at a geometric rate. Not only that, but the subsequent course of events has been described as an 'educational explosion', and rightly so. By the mid-1960s, when the incidence of *studentexamen* was supposed to have levelled off, the acceleration was greater than ever. Far from stagnating, new admissions to the arts and science faculties increased sharply. The number of pupils with so-called academic choices grew apace, specially after the basic school reform of 1962, so that the proportion of pupils making such choices rose to more than two-thirds from about one-third during the 1950s. With the introduction of a universal basic school in 1962, followed by reforms of secondary education in 1964, the educational opportunities were expanded far beyond the prospects envisaged in 1958, and all the earlier forecasts were shattered into the bargain. The predicted surplus of Swedish and modern language teachers in the early 1960s was never realized. As for the liberal arts graduates, the much talked about surplus turned out to be a hampering shortage, which prevailed until the beginning of the 1970s when a (rather unexpected) surplus of all kinds of teachers began to haunt the country.

I have not picked out this example in order to act wise after the event, but because I feel that a generous helping of imagination is called for when one tries to extrapolate development trends. In this particular case the acceleration tendencies which already existed ought to have given people cause to think about the role of education both as investment and consumption, and hence about its attractiveness as well. If such reflections had been allowed to govern, the forecasts could have been corrected. It should also have been possible to predict the short-range effects of broadened educational opportunities as well as the temptation to produce an over-supply.

(3) Social and political values are legitimate objects of research for the futurologist. For example, he can study how pluralistic and monolithic societies respectively function in educational terms. However, the futurologist cannot avoid being drawn into the debate about what kind of future society is being sought. In so doing he can indirectly help to create values and gain their wider adoption. The appearance of tomorrow's society does not follow in any clear-cut and mechanical way from the scientific and technological potentials we have today, and probably not from the ones at our command tomorrow, either. The crux is *if* and *how* we intend to use these potentials. That is determined by the social preferences, i.e., by the prevailing values. Medical science can give us formulas on leading a way of life that will keep us in good shape physically and mentally. But none the less we put ourselves in situations, both on and off the job, that induce stress and break us down physically and mentally. We allow the waste products of technology to spoil our environment to the stage where it poses health hazards not only for coming generations but also for ourselves.

Will the values that fix priorities and preferences look essentially different two or three decades from now? Will science and technology be harnessed more towards creating a better and healthier environment? And what about notions as to what constitutes the 'good' life, the life worth living? The protestant ethic (*pace* Max Weber), under which everyone was supposed to stick to his last, and which suffused the life ideal of a large part of my generation in the Western world (and in the socialist countries, too, for that matter), may be superseded by another ethic. As long as the 'sweat it out' ethic dominates, the awarding of marks on the basis of individual performances in competition will continue to dominate our schools. The curricula can then talk as piously as they want about group work, co-operation, consideration and social maturity.

Many signs suggest that here, as in so many other areas, the revolt of youth is touching off what Nietzsche called a 'reappraisal of all values'. Thus we have a growing younger generation who oppose the toiling philosophy of their elders and who no longer want to give top priority to traditional status-promoting achievements in school and in the job world. Obviously such a reappraisal cannot help but strongly influence the school's assessment of the progress its pupils are making.

Hence one of the cardinal tasks for futurology will be to venture predictions about how priorities are going to look in another few decades. What will then be considered essential and inessential? What will one be living for? All of us have personal experiences of how the value accents can shift in a relatively short time. My own generation was not confronted with the problems that relate to the atomic bomb and the developing countries. We rested, if not securely then ingenuously, in the assurance that the Western way of life was superior and our technical civilization unbeatable. There was no talk of technology being able to harm us in any way; it could only make life richer, better and elevate us to higher and higher standards of living.

I do not propose here to elaborate on how one

undertakes to find out about tomorrow's value priorities. If we look at what has happened to change social and political values during the past century, we often detect certain advance signals of what is in store where needs and values are concerned. Such a study will disclose that events constantly thrust up avant-gardists, many of them leading writers, whose ideas and reactions portend the coming shape of dominant values. These signals that point ahead to the future are to be found among writers, artists and intellectuals, but even more so among articulate young people.

These young people will take over the society of tomorrow. By investigating what they hold to be questions of vital importance, we can arrive at a broader understanding not only of what they as young people accord top priority, but also of what they may be expected to consider most essential in their adult years. The Swedish National Board of Education recently published an attitude survey whose main purpose was to provide source data for instruction in religion. A questionnaire administered to 1,300 pupils in grade 9 showed that racial problems, international problems and questions of human dignity headed the list of philosophical and ethical topics which concerned pupils at the age of sixteen.

The American investigators who concern themselves with educational policy research have made extremely interesting attempts to map out how vital questions are perceived by more articulate and 'deviant' youth respectively. A group of high school students, all of them engaged in putting out 'underground' school newspapers, were invited to a conference where they gave uninhibited expression to their views of the older generation and the existing society, and portrayed the kind of society they would like to have in the future. Another study included the 'hippies' of San Francisco. A third tied in to an ongoing international study in twenty-five countries which seeks to elucidate the value orientations, attitudes and political opinions of university undergraduates.

When I read the analysis of the taped proceedings from the conference attended by the young high school editors, I could not escape the reflection that young people now seem to be reacting in the same way more or less universally. After all, these are individuals who experience the world and its problems more directly and tangibly, not least through the medium of television, than earlier generations, and for whom there exist quite different means than in the past for the common sharing of experience.

According to these youngsters, the school is out of touch with the important things that are happening in the world and is also trying to protect the pupils against unpleasant realities. They consider themselves 'manipulated', with the school acting as a propaganda machine. One of them said, 'The school system has become an efficient factory in which we are the raw material, who under the pressure of the marking system are turned into automatons and conformists for sale to the highest bidders in the business world.' Another student said, 'What I want more than anything else in the school is interaction between ideas and feelings, and not just neutral, grey knowledge. I want us to get accustomed to people trying to convince us about things.'

I should like to comment briefly on both these quotations, since I picked them out in order to illustrate a favourite idea of mine. The day cannot be far off when we stop adhering to the illusion that textbooks or teaching aids in general are supposed to present 'objective' knowledge. Efforts in that direction make the books so neutral and dull that they cannot possibly stimulate the motivation of pupils. The latter-day debate in Sweden, for instance, about the tacit value assumptions in the textbooks has shown us that we must try another approach. Quite simply this means that pupils must be put in touch with the debate and clash of opinions in the larger society outside the school: in other words, that the school must systematically expose its pupils to these views and train them in their discussion. We shall be living in a society where intentions are becoming more important than opinions.

Futurology, not least that concerned with development trends under alternative 2, confronts this crucial question: what trends shall be selected for extrapolation? Some of these trends will be decisively influenced by a policy based on future assessments of priorities. Other trends will probably remain more stable. It therefore becomes essential to design 'alternative futures', all according to the congeries of assumptions one makes.

As for the type of society represented by the industrial countries, it is likely that several of these trends will be reinforced in the future. Just how they will develop mathematically, i.e. linearly or exponentially, will depend *inter alia* on the future's value preferences.

We cannot devise sensible future alternatives unless two fundamental conditions are in hand: (1) we regard education as an integrated system, which means we do not confine ourselves to the school-type subsystems in the conventional sense; and (2) we view the educational system in its social, economic and political context. What this boils down to is an attempt to design 'comprehensive' future alternatives.

The factors which characterize the educational system as such are here called endogenous, whereas those influences which derive from the total social context are called exogenous. Accordingly, efforts to design alternative futures must embrace certain assumptions (more or less correlated with one another) concerning both kinds of factors, on the one hand assumptions about society at large and on the other about the educational system as such.

Assumptions about society at large

(1) Economic growth will offer opportunities for increased consumption in different respects (better material standards, more leisure, more education and culture).

(2) The process of change will accelerate in essential respects, e.g. in the manufacture of goods and the provision of services.

(3) Greater international exposure is to be expected by virtue of mass media and travel.

(4) An accelerating flow of information will have to be coped with both on the production side (scientific research) and on the distribution side (mass media, computer technology).

(5) Gainful employment as a means of obtaining life's necessities will become increasingly unimportant. An overabundance of goods and services in the highly industrialized countries will be available to the masses.

(6) Increased influence for experts, with a tendency towards meritocracy.

(7) Increased pluralism, at least for a transitional period, as regards life outlooks and values.

(8) It will be increasingly difficult to maintain a balance between the ecological system and technology (owing to pollution and ravages of nature).

These assumptions obviously present varying degrees of plausibility. The first four appear to intercorrelate highly and their current manifestations are so patent that they should be considered very plausible. By contrast, the four last assumptions are more debatable, one reason being that contemporary values will supposedly carry over by and large to the future — for example, that education will continue to be a strong status-promoting factor, or that technological advances which make for greater benefits now are bought at the price of tomorrow's devastation. To my mind, the most debatable assumption is the one about increased pluralism.

General assumptions about the educational system

Now, what assumptions can we make about the future educational system? Before going into details, I should like to single out what ought to be regarded as the most important overlapping conditions for tomorrow's learning society, where it will become increasingly urgent to work out 'systems solutions' and not merely short-range partial solutions. Three such conditions make it particularly important to formulate systems solutions, namely (1) the enrolment explosion, the increased proportions of more and more cohorts who are going in for full-time education; (2) the knowledge explosion, which aggravates the problem of processing, storing and retrieving information; and (3) the need to individualize instruction, i.e. to enable every individual to learn at the pace and with the breadth and depth that suit him best, in short the demand for greater specificity in the process of imparting knowledge and skills. Individualization in our schools will soon become a necessity, not a luxury as heretofore.

Now, what can be specifically assumed about the future educational system that looks more or less plausible?

(1) Education is going to be a lifelong process. The type of school associated with youth will not provide the fare on which one can subsist for all time.

(2) Education will not have clearly defined 'cut-offs' as in the past, beginning with an entrance examination and ending with a near-dramatic climax such as a secondary school examination or a university degree. It will become more of a continuous process, both as regards its effluxion over time and its embedment in the other functions of life.

(3) Education will take on a more informal character as it

becomes accessible to more and more individuals. In addition to 'learning centres', facilities will be provided for learning at home and at the workplace, for example by the installation of terminals.

(4) Formal education of the type that used to take place in conventional school plants will, as it becomes accessible to more and more individuals, also become more meaningful and relevant in terms of its application.

(5) To an ever increasing extent, the educational system will become dependent on large supporting organizations or supporting systems. Agencies of this kind, whether they be public or private, are needed to produce systems of teaching aids, systems of information processing and multi-media instructional materials. The information systems arrived at will consist of carefully tried and tested storage and retrieval components. One of the problems involved will be to create 'compatibility' between medium and receiver.

For me it stood out as fairly self-evident more than ten years ago that the basic school of the future would have to concentrate on inculcating certain fundamental learning skills. It would have to impart skills and knowledge for two purposes: to train for general citizenship and to qualify the young for the initial training needed for certain occupations. Further, it would have to prepare the young for changing careers, for instance by providing a basic repertoire of skills as well as attitudes of flexibility and a taste for more, a motivation for going on with education.

In the light of these remarks, the following objectives strike me as paramount. Some of them may be regarded as controversial because they proceed from values which also form part and parcel of political judgements.

(1) It will be increasingly important for democracy to create the broadest possible frame of reference for knowledge, skills and attitudes. The production and use of

information will become more and more specialized. This will readily lead to rule by specialists and experts, which brings formalism and alienation in its train. At the same time as scientific research and high-level education become increasingly important to society, the merits attached to them increase concomitantly. We seem to be headed towards a meritocracy. Among other things, a common frame of reference means making initial provision for a common liberal schooling to the greatest extent, with vocationally oriented specialization to follow much later. The development of communications skills should be emphasized so greatly that the maximum number of citizens will be enabled to speak the same language and hence understand one another.

(2) Basic schooling ought to be of the kind that lays the groundwork for re-educability, for instance by providing what was referred to above as an adequate basic repertoire of skills and the ability to assimilate further knowledge.

(3) The school ought to instil receptivity to change, in other words a flexible attitude conducive to a willingness to go ahead both with general education and vocational training. It should get across a realization that the whole of life will be one long continuation school.

(4) The school must prepare its pupils to live in a society of pluralistic values. Among other things, this means developing individual ability to pick and choose on the basis of certain criteria of authenticity.

(5) Schooling for internationalism and the defeat of present-day educational provincialism is necessary if the world is going to survive.

(6) It will be necessary to build up skills to deal with the ever more torrential flow of information unless we are to be swept away by it. Among these skills are computer language and technology.

(7) Schooling for a life where gainful employment and

recreation (in the old sense) will become less and less important, and where 'work' will increasingly take on the character of self-realization.

(8) Schooling for comprehension of the importance of maintaining the ecological system and technology in balance (involving the whole complex of problems which relate to such things as pollution of air, water and soil, and the wanton exploitation of natural resources).

(9) Schooling in the ability to live as an independent individual, without necessarily having to rely on support in some primary group such as the family.

As I see it, a crucial aspect will be the extent to which education is going to function as a social mobility factor. Will it become increasingly important as a determinant of status (to judge from current tendencies)? Must we anticipate that the educational system, as regards its school-type subsystems, will remain pretty much institutionalized? If so, the outlook is for greater bureaucratization in that the system will be run by an establishment of highly educated technocrats.

Specific assumptions about education

(1) General education and vocational training will be more and more interwoven, simply because it will not be possible to predict what specific vocational attainments will be needed in the future. Paradoxically, general education (in the form of a 'basic repertoire' of fundamental skills and knowledge) will be the best kind of vocational training. Basic schooling will constitute the foundation for re-educability.

(2) Basic schooling will aim to accommodate the broadest possible common frame of reference of knowledge, skills and attitudes to cope with an era of ever increasing specialization.

(3) Skills (above all those which help in the assimilation of

knowledge) will acquire greater importance at the expense of specific pieces of information. It will be impossible to uphold the traditional encyclopedic ideal of education.

(4) Instruction will become more and more individualized (for instance as more technical resources are brought into play). Teachers will be 'replaceable' by technical aids to a limited extent only, since the central element of pedagogical activity is the personal contact between teacher and pupil. The teacher's duties will be to plan, support and evaluate the course of progress for the individual pupil.

(5) The educative role in the wide sense of the school (as an institution) will decline in importance as increased leisure confers greater influence on the family and the peer group. Mass media will extend their influence, and television especially so by virtue of lengthened transmission times and an increased number of channels.

(6) Education in the formal schooling sense tends to become more expensive. Since more and more young people (and adults) are studying, while annual costs per pupil are rising concurrently, it appears that the margin set by the overall allocation of resources will soon become so narrow that far-reaching rationalizations will have to be put into effect in order to achieve a more efficient utilization of resources. These may be expected to alter fundamental aspects of the school as an institution. This is likely to have radical repercussions on the erection of school buildings, since their design inevitably proceeds from assumptions about the uses of these buildings for several decades to come.

Now it may be asked: isn't everything that is supposed to happen happening anyway, regardless of our hopes for the future and our efforts to enlist the help of research towards imbuing the actual development process with an

air of rationality? Can futurology help to create the future?
It might seem as though many technicians and politicians
are acting — or failing to act — after the principle of
'*après moi le déluge*'. Fagerberg has very aptly affixed the
label of 'no-motion Messiah' to this mentality. I trust I am
not indulging in lax quasi-philosophizing when I say that
the hallmark of contemporary man is his conviction that he
can choose and shape his own future. The traditional run
of humanity naturally saw itself as caught up in an
unpremeditated and fated historical process, and
considered its sole purpose on earth to continue, repeat
and reproduce the life that earlier generations had lived.
In spite of everything, contemporary man is inspired by the
optimistic conviction that he holds the future in his hands.
In spite of everything, he entertains the hope that he will
be able to write the 'scenario' for his own life and for the
lives of his descendants. Indeed, he goes so far as to hope
that he will be able to stage the drama of life in
accordance with the scenario's directions.

2 Can teaching aids replace the teacher?

The 1961 Congress of the International Association of Applied Psychology, which was held in Copenhagen, gave ample space on its agenda to the latest American-spawned 'gimmicks' in education: programmed instruction and teaching machines. In a discussion that followed one of the lectures, a member of the audience, evidently a teacher, anxiously wondered whether the new machines were meant to replace the teaching profession. The lecturer to whom this question was put happened, if I remember correctly, to be Professor Robert Glaser of Pittsburgh University, who now heads its Learning Research and Development Centre. Professor Glaser is a pioneer of research into individualized learning and the role that technical aids can play in this process. The audience was struck dumb by the succinctness of his reply: 'A teacher who can be replaced by a machine ought to be.' Since these words also answer the question asked in the title of this essay, I should perhaps stop here and not impose any further on the reader's time. But because the problem also has other aspects that are worth discussing, I shall make so bold as to proceed nevertheless. So that the platform on which the following thoughts rest may be understood, I should like to say that my answer to the title question goes like this: in so far as the teacher cannot be replaced by teaching aids, that will be because they should, on educational and economic grounds, supplement him. But they should also emancipate him in that they give him the opportunity to perform those duties which are central to his mission.

I have said it before and I say it again: the school's 'methods of production' date from a pre-industrial era. By and large our schools still inculcate knowledge and skills in the ways they did fifty or one hundred years ago, for all the 'progressive' efforts to renew methods and improve efficiency. Large segments of manufacturing industry have long been spending much more on tools and machinery than on buildings, but investment in educational plant still accords a modest share to auxiliary devices for instruction. Obviously, the parallel between school and industry should not be drawn too closely. The inculcation of knowledge and skills is not the same as the manufacture or distribution of material products. But whereas industry has increasingly adopted technical aids to replace manpower or to amplify human muscle, the school more or less treats the new teaching aids as foreign bodies that have yet to be integrated into its organism. The investigations that have been made of what now goes on in an ordinary classroom have unanimously shown that the actual teaching process (I refrain from using the euphemism 'attempts to create conditions for the conduct of teaching') is unalloyed class or 'frontal' instruction. The teacher lectures to his class. He asks questions and calls on individual pupils to answer them. As a rule, self-activity and independent work by the pupils is extremely limited.

Should we now set out to explore how school work can be made more efficient with the use of teaching aids, a first step must be to analyse the objectives and the conditions under which learning takes place. Such an analysis ought to provide reference points for an assessment of the influences at work in changing the teacher's role, not only in the school of today but also in the school of tomorrow. There is not much point in discussing the use of aids in school work unless we view them as integral parts of a work process that is changing in character, and which implies that the roles of both teacher and pupil are being transformed.

An overriding objective of formal education in modern society is 'teaching pupils to learn', to lay a foundation for the lifelong schooling that must come into being if people are to cope with the imperatives of constant change. It is no longer a question of having the teacher mainly serve as a communicator of 'solid facts'. For various reasons, not least the findings of research, the life of a solid fact in our time is brutally short, and growing shorter. The major objective, therefore, is to teach pupils to acquire knowledge on their own. From this it follows that the main things to teach are fundamental concepts, principles, key terms and ways of looking at a subject. The subject areas themselves should be learned as basic disciplines which are involved in constant change, but whose essential intellectual structures show longer durability.

The foregoing observations apply not only to the generally educational aspect of formal schooling, but also to vocational training. Henceforth this must not chiefly aim at imparting knowledge of or skills in specifc trades, but at training us to acquire useful skills, to modify them and – not least – to begin again from the beginning. Adaptability and flexibility are basic qualities demanded of the men and women in today's labour force.

Sooner or later the objectives of a school that educates pupils for tomorrow's society are bound to react on its work practices, and hence also promote the use of aids that will not only facilitate the communication of knowledge and skills but also enable the teacher to give more of himself to the important aspects of this process. Teaching cannot merely consist of talking to the class as a whole, giving everybody the same homework, putting questions to individual pupils and administering tests. If these are supposed to be the central functions, then we can immediately establish that teaching and learning are far from being identical. In the first place, it cannot be taken for granted that the taught are learning anything. In extreme cases they do not learn anything at all. In the second place, the pupil may still be able to learn a great deal even if he is not subjected to any formal instruction.

Much of that which occurs in the process we call teaching rests upon two premises, which are usually not made explicit. The first is that the pupil learns something not because it is attractive or pleasing, but to avoid disagreeable consequences if he does not learn it. To get him to learn he must be made to feel the threat of censure, low marks, non-promotion and the like. The second premise is that the teacher is the *primus motor* who keeps the pupils going. He hands out the lessons and makes sure his pupils do them. No essential spontaneous learning activity on the pupil's part is assumed. He is often conceived as the unwilling recipient of the knowledge that the teacher transmits to him.

The somewhat caricatured picture of the teaching process given above represents what I like to call the 'drinking-glass model'. In place of glasses, read pupils, and in place of water read wisdom, which is what the teacher pours out of his pitcher. It could also be called the Medusa model, because the motivation theory it embodies assumes the teacher to incarnate the unpleasantness that pupils want to avoid, such as censure and the threat of bad marks. Unpleasantness is considered essential, or even indispensable, for learning.

Even the slightest familiarity with educational psychology will tell us that those two inexplicit premises are way off base. Whatever else they may be, they are not crucial determinants of learning. The primary determinant is positive motivation. Subject matter – and there is a great deal of it – for which the pupil has not felt even a modicum of original need must be 'embedded' in a larger, more positive context, for example the prospect of being commended for what one does, or the hope that a distasteful preoccupation of the moment will eventuate in some sort of ultimate reward. But if the pupil spends the greater part of his day on tasks he doesn't want to do, the reward is bound to be small or nil. A teacher who is not assailed by doubts about his own performance ought to ask himself the following questions: do my pupils stop working as soon as I say the lesson is over? Do I reward my pupils for good work by exempting them from other tasks? Do I give them extra work as punishment? Unless I give them homework to do, will they spontaneously undertake tasks in my subject? Do I praise them when they broach points of view that differ from those presented by me or the textbook?

Pupils do not learn from the teacher, but on the basis of factors that exist inside themselves. In the final analysis, the activity on which schooling depends springs from the pupils. They are the ones who do the learning. The teacher's task is to create the conditions which will make that learning as effective as possible. No one is going to learn simply because somebody tells him to: that fact is basic. An incentive must be generated to activate the pupil's motivation to learn. The incentive may lie in the subject matter to be learned. But it may also lie in the actual method of working: in the opportunities for activity, creativeness and independence which it offers. Here is where teaching aids can really be instrumental in educational strategy, quite apart from the fact that they save the teacher's time.

In our age of flux, compounded by technological advance and the knowledge explosion, the teacher's role is inevitably affected. Its ongoing transformation may be briefly described as follows. These days the teacher is not so much a fountainhead of knowledge as a man who taps its sources and guides his pupils to them. It is he who mobilizes the information, the material to be learned. To avoid misunderstanding, I should hasten to add that this obviously does not require today's teachers to know less about their subjects than their forerunners did. On the contrary, the growing corpus of knowledge in different subjects will inexorably compel them not only to specialize, but also to add breadth and depth to their presentation of segments within the general subject field.

First and foremost the teacher must give more of himself to the organization of learning opportunities for the individual pupil. This means that his role will be less didactic, i.e. intended to convey instruction directly to the class as a whole, and more individualizing, i.e. it will ensure that every pupil most appropriately acquires the knowledge and skills which he can acquire under the existing conditions.

It is against this background, admittedly painted in very broad strokes, that one should discuss how modern teaching aids can replace, supplement and release the teacher. I am well aware that the case for introducing teacher-saving devices can be argued by the increased need for teachers, the shortage of qualified staff and, not least, the demands for economizing on this manpower. My reflections will mainly pertain to what teaching aids can do to economize on instruction time and to produce better learning opportunities. They do not conflict in principle with the endeavours that stem from purely economic motives.

It will have emerged from the foregoing that the instructional ideal is total individualization. The educational researcher may be forgiven if, in his more ecstatic moments, he envisages the teacher as a physician who, after having made his individual diagnosis, writes out the best prescription for a pupil and tells him to have it filled out by a pharmacy of tried and tested didactic alternatives. That may strike many as talking about champagne when the best that can be offered in the practical school situation is small beer. None the less, I shall venture to elaborate this vision below because it ought to guide us when we cross the threshold leading to the 'industrial' era that also lies ahead of the school. The ideal must be to aim at giving every pupil the advantage formerly vouchsafed to the aristocracy alone, namely to have a tutor at his side. After all, why not emulate Philip of Macedonia, who gave his son Alexander an Aristotle?

That smacks of champagne indeed, but how do we go about distilling this fine brew? Such visions by themselves may perhaps only embitter those tired teachers who spend their afternoons and evenings preparing materials that will impart some individualizing dimension to their lessons. As I see it, the didactic revolution implied by radical individualization can only be achieved if 'material-methods systems' are worked out in the different subject fields. Suffice it here to point out that this activity will require the consolidated capabilities of methods specialists, subject matter specialists and behavioural scientists, plus some millions of kronor out of public funds. We can no longer surrender to the meaningless hopes that piously worded curriculum prescriptions and preachments about methodic renewal in the education and training of teachers will have decisive effects on the individual teacher and his work in the classroom. The conditions under which he works today afford very little scope for the individualization about which so many lofty words have been spoken.

For the purposes of my discourse, I shall disregard aids of the type that reify teaching or that have customarily formed integral parts of it, such as textbooks, slide projectors, charts and the like. Instead, I shall concentrate on the newer aids that are not only more sparing of the teacher's time but also permit more active and economical learning. A distinguishing feature of these aids is that they operate in the learning situation without any effort from the teacher other than planning their use. They are also distinguished by their ability to communicate subject matter whose methodic arrangement and sequencing would otherwise require enormous inputs of work, not least by educational expertise, but where every pupil can be theoretically raised to the status of an Alexander, with an Aristotle as his teacher.

Let me begin with those aids which are solely intended for skill-building, such as learning studios and self-instruction materials gradated by difficulty. An example of the latter is the so-called SIM material (self-instructional material), which is currently used in our country to teach Swedish in the last grades of the basic school. It comprises a large number of non-fiction prose texts that have been thoroughly tested and fitted with problem exercises. Every pupil starts out by taking a diagnostic test, which determines the difficulty level which suits him best. Since a copious selection of texts is available at every level, he can also work with material that falls within his sphere of interest.

From there on he is successively 'promoted' to higher levels of difficulty according to the progress he makes. Because the material is self-correcting, the teacher is on hand mostly to perform as diagnostician and administrator. It should immediately be pointed out that this technique in no way 'replaces' the teacher. First of all, the material cannot encompass the whole subject field but only, as in this case, a subskill in the vast and complex subject of the mother tongue. Second, the skill-building and sheer communication of knowledge involved demands a great deal of interaction between teacher and pupil.

Further development of material-methods systems, especially in secondary education, should substantially reduce the number of lessons as fixed by weekly room schedules, and offer correspondingly greater scope for the pupil's independent work, even though that will largely have to be performed in the school plant itself, at least within the foreseeable future. The point at issue here, put perhaps in extreme form, is this: some pupils never get the opportunity to learn what they can or want to learn, for all the teaching they have to put up with! If more independent work is to be fostered, it is necessary not only to produce skill-building material of the type represented by SIM, but also textbook kits with collateral readings and teacher manuals that permit independent and individualized study. Thus, in a subject like civics, various public affairs could be illuminated with a system of materials collected in booklets and worksheets, which tie in with a guide that tells the pupil where they are to be found and how they should be read, but at the same time leaves considerable leeway for individual interests.

So far I have confined myself mainly to printed aids which link up with the tradition we already have with textbooks and exercise booklets in the school. The basic innovation the materials entail is that their design requires a massive and co-ordinated effort by specialists at the national level. During the past ten years experiments have commenced with technical aids that open up dazzling vistas for future education. In 1954 the Harvard psychologist B. F. Skinner published an article in which he developed the idea of a new teaching technology based on his many years of research into the learning process. A few years later the first 'teaching machines' made their debut. Curiously, the first real instruction programmes came out somewhat later. But of these as of so many other technical aids, the now familiar rule is that it is easier, and above all much faster, to produce the machines than the pedagogical miracles that the machines are called upon to perform.

Whether the programmed aids exist only in the form of printed material that resembles textbooks or are conveyed by machines, they build upon two principles. The one is immediate reinforcement. A pupil promptly finds out if he has answered rightly or wrongly, an outcome that in the classroom usually befalls only the pupil who happens to have the question put to him. When a whole class is working on the same exercise, the reinforcement comes long after the answer is available, i.e. not until the teacher has corrected the material. The first attempts with programming were made in straight skill subjects; programmes for learning the basic algorisms of arithmetic are an example. The second principle is that the pupil is advanced in small steps to lessen the risk of erroneous responses, and thereby keep him from getting discouraged. These two basic principles of programmed instruction make possible much better individualization than the scope of ordinary classroom teaching allows.

It is evident, however, that the programmed aids we have had up to now are far from ideal as individualizing instruments. Most of the programmes are 'linear', which means having every pupil go through all the material. For brighter pupils that requirement can be rather tedious, especially if the steps of difficulty are very small. But the biggest drawback is the rigid relationship between the pupil on the one hand, and the material and device on the other. Thus only a few 'branching' programmes have permitted the assignment of different routes to the pupils according to the progress they achieve. However, both these problems have been amenable to technical solution through the use of computers.

The first experiments with computerized instruction began around 1960 — if I remember correctly, at the Systems Development Corporation in Santa Monica, California. Since then the experiments have proliferated, spurred on by heavy investments of technical, pedagogical and financial resources. To the best of my knowledge, the place that has come furthest is Stanford University, where a research team under Professor Patrick Suppes has spent several years on developing computer-based programmes in mathematics for grades 3 to 8. The computer helps to maximize individualization by offering two basic advantages. First, it can be programmed to follow every pupil not only in a class but also in one or more schools, which it does by storing every single response from the pupil; secondly, according to the incidence of right and wrong answers, it can select the next lessons which best serve that particular pupil. Whenever the teacher feels like it he can retrieve from the computer all the information he needs about his class or classes, or about the individual pupil. According to Professor Suppes, the main problems of computerized instruction are not technical but educational: how to develop individualizing methods and shape the subject matter to make it suit the individual pupil rather than groups of pupils.

So as to convey a more concrete picture of what this is all about, I shall briefly describe the technical equipment that Professor Suppes uses in his experiments. This has been advanced to the point where a number of terminals installed at a school in East Palo Alto are hooked up to a computer at the Stanford computation centre. The pupil is seated in front of a cathode ray tube that resembles the screen on a television set. On this screen the computer displays the pictures, words, diagrams and figures that go into the pupil's lesson materials. In addition to the cathode ray tube an electric typewriter is available which the pupil can use for his responses. The typewriter is actuated by the computer to print messages that tell the pupil not only whether he has done right or wrong, but also what sort of mistakes he has made. The pupil also has access to a special pen that he can point with on the screen to designate different alternatives or parts; he need not restrict his answer to the typewriter. Lastly, Professor Suppes uses an earphone to transmit programmed recorded messages to the pupil – an especially important feature when the listeners are young children.

The mathematics programme for grades 5 and 6 is graduated at five levels of difficulty. Depending on how the pupil performs, the computer directs him from one level to another. If he answers correctly more than 80 per cent of the lesson problems at one level, he is moved up to the next level. If his correct answers fall below 60 per cent, he is moved down to a lower level.

Now it must not be believed that the whole mathematics course is learned in this way. Computer-assisted instruction is used only in short passes of ten to fifteen minutes to practise the concepts and operations that the teacher has gone through orally with the class beforehand. However, the very fact that a machine can handle almost the whole follow-up of a pupil's skill-building represents an enormous advance.

The next stage in computerized instruction has been to devise programmes that will enable the computer to function as teacher for the individual pupil, i.e. as his private tutor. Those who are familiar with the layout of programmed textbooks know that fundamental concepts and theorems are also adaptable to programmed learning. In principle, therefore, a computer can be made to take over the presentation of such subject matter in conformity with a programme that is designed for it.

All the same, not even the most sanguine optimists believe in easy solutions of the problems that must be solved in order to achieve a real 'dialogue' between machine and pupil. One of these problems is to get the computer to respond adequately to human speech. But even if that problem can be solved, the computer still cannot replace the teacher because there remains the central educational mission consisting in the direct personal relationship between teacher and pupil. As I have said, the ideal role for the teacher *qua* teacher ought to emphasize the planning and guidance of learning by the individual pupil. Even so, and without resort to any pathetic appeals on our part, there is no getting away from the fact that the teacher's duties far transcend the 'organization of learning opportunities'. He must mediate the contacts of growing people with the adult culture, act as a model, as a creator of ideals – in truth, tasks that are anything but easy in an age of pluralistic values such as ours. All those noble words in printed curricula about the teacher's educative duties will readily tend to remain visions of champagne unless practical arrangements are made to enable him to devote more of himself to planning the individual pupil's road through courses and stages – unless he is released from the kind of work that other sectors of the national life entrusted to technology a long time ago.

The educational sector does not occupy a place so far apart from the rest as to justify denying its practitioners the benefits of technological advance. The use of technical aids in industry has not turned people into slaves of machines. On the contrary, these aids have increasingly assumed the unskilled and semiskilled tasks that have degraded human labour. In consequence, the remaining inputs of human effort have increasingly become highly skilled. To that extent the aids have not replaced manpower but have liberated it, the better to provide scope for the more genuine and central tasks of the teaching profession.

Educational planning 3

Up to the early 1950s the majority of economists, administrators and politicians looked upon education, unless it was clear-cut preparation for specific vocations, as consumption pure and simple. Higher education, especially in the liberal arts departments of universities, was widely regarded together with research as an exclusive luxury, roughly on a par with the exercise of artistic and literary talents. The exclusiveness was further underlined by the fact that access to such education was greatly hedged in with economic and social barriers. To travesty what Kolingen[1] once said about the toothbrush, education at higher levels was a form of 'self-indulgence for the upper class'. The old mercantilist system, which put a premium on the cultivation of 'genius', cherished a belief not only in talent as such but also in adequately nurtured talent as an investment. In the United States, a pragmatic view of the school's mission took an early hold. When the great wave of immigrants began to pour in over the country during the second half of the nineteenth century,

[1] Kolingen was a cartoon tramp of gentlemanly pretensions who figured prominently in early twentieth-century Swedish caricature. 1969 was the 100th anniversary of the birth of his creator, Albert Engström (1869–1940).

the overriding function imputed to the school was to Americanize all these people with their motley ethnic background. From about the turn of the century, reform movements both in Europe and the US saw the tax-supported public school as an instrument to impart fundamental skills to the working men who were needed to man a rapidly expanding industry. This way of looking at things was especially pronounced in the US.

But as we said it was not until the 1950s that social scientists began to look upon education not only as consumption but also as an investment which promotes economic growth. This could not be solely explained by the two factors of classical economics, the supply of physical capital and labour reported as statistical units, and where the latter was concerned without regard for its quality. Economic growth was essentially derived from the general education and the vocational training which labour obtained, i.e. by investment in human capital, and from the research which served to improve the quality of physical capital. The forerunners in this school of thought were economists such as Theodore Schultz in the US, Friedrich Edding in Germany and Ingvar Svennilson in Sweden.

Methods to measure expansion of the 'knowledge industry'

Two leading experts in the discipline that in America goes under the name 'economics of education', Frederick Harbison and Charles Myers, have described 'strategies for the development of human resources' in their book, *Education, Manpower and Economic Growth* (1964). The reference here is to the increment of knowledge and skills which generally takes place in a given society. Three types of development factors are identified: (1) formal schooling, with the main emphasis usually on a general and liberal education; (2) adult education, both in and out of working life; and (3) 'self-improvement' in the form of correspondence courses and similar private studies, and, furthermore, better hygiene and dietary habits in the interests of improved health.

The 'knowledge industry', to use a term coined by Fritz Machlup (who made it cover both the production of knowledge with the help of research and its distribution by means of education), is currently expanding at almost twice the rate for industry as a whole.

Studies of the relationship between education and economic growth have employed methods that fall into four main classes as follows:

(1) In the 1950s Theodore Schultz of Chicago devised a method which he called the 'rate-of-return approach', i.e. an attempt to measure the yield of money invested in education. Since 1963, when he published his book, *The Economic Value of Education*, there has been considerable research into the return that accrues from such investment to both the individual and the community at large. Schultz himself has contributed to attempts to estimate the role of education in general economic growth.

To gauge the attractiveness of education as an investment object in the US, Schultz worked out estimates for the period from 1900 to 1956. In terms of constant dollars the resources put into education during this period were found to have increased three and a half times in relation to consumer incomes and also to physical capital formation. In other words, education as an investment has proved to be three and a half times more attractive than physical capital.

(2) The so-called residual method, where the aim is to measure the proportions of economic growth during a period that are respectively attributable to input of capital and labour (in statistical units). The

unexplained remainder (or 'residual') is accordingly attributed to the improved quality resulting from education and research. Aukrust in Norway is one of the economists who has worked with this method.

(3) A common method has been to estimate both the individual and social rates of return from education. By building upon data about the incomes earned by persons of varying educational levels and about what they and society have spent on their education, an investigator can obtain measures of the return for the individual and society at large. Garry Becker has estimated the return on capital invested in a college education and comes up with a rate of 10–12 per cent. Attempts have also been made to estimate the present value of a specified course by finding out about the aggregate life income.

(4) A method used by Friedrich Edding, Ingvar Svennilson and Lionel Elvin in a publication prepared for the OECD is to determine the correlation between national product per capita in different countries and their school enrolments at different levels. Eddings arrived at a rank order correlation coefficient of +0·90, which is very high. The correlation, obviously, applies to whole countries and not to individuals and is, as is the case with correlations between series of aggregates, spuriously high.

Now it should be immediately pointed out, as indeed Harbison and Myers have also done, that the economic return from education cannot be calculated in the same way as for a factory or irrigation dam. However we look at education, some part of it must be regarded as consumption – it 'improves the mind'. Taking all things together, man does not live by bread alone – no more so than he lives by intellectual nourishment alone.

By virtue of the strategic role that education has come to play in the advanced industrial countries, it has come to be an article very much in demand, the more so since these countries are caught up in their second industrial revolution under the aegis of electronics and cybernetics. Whereas back in the 1930s the educated man was likely to run the same if not actually greater risk of unemployment than the uneducated in a stagnant and deflationary economy, the situation is now completely changed. In the United States a university degree is soon predicted for one of every four employees, and a shortage of people with this attainment is expected for certain graduates. At the same time most of the unemployment will be confined to those with a substratum of formal schooling so slight that it cannot substain the retraining for skilled occupations that would put them back into the labour market.

Examples from the industrialized world have spurred the developing countries to go at the expansion of their formal school systems with abandoned enthusiasm. The plans that have been worked out for literary campaigns, partly under the auspices of UNESCO, are extremely ambitious — according to some, unrealistically ambitious. A global perspective of the 'educational explosion' may be formed when we consider that, from 1950 to 1965, the world's educational establishments admitted as many for full-time tuition as during the past 1,000 years! This explosion has necessitated planning programmes relating not only to the educational systems of individual countries, but also to the international technical assistance in the sphere of education that has grown so strongly in the past two decades.

Planning the educational system in its entirety

All planning of the kind here at issue involves trying to establish priorities in a situation of limited resources. In the past few decades expenditures on education have risen universally, both in relation to size of national products and the total receipts of governments. There is also a tendency, most pronounced in the affluent countries, for costs per pupil and year to rise in constant money values, which reflects not only measures for the quantitative improvement of education but also – and perhaps more significantly – rising standards of living. Where developing countries are concerned, relating the expenditures on education to the national product does not tell us very much; they should be chiefly compared with the total expenditures in the public sector. For many developing countries that sector does not exceed perhaps 10 per cent of the national product, which means that mounting educational programmes impose much greater burdens on them in relative terms; Latin America is a particular case in point.

In an article published some years ago, Philip H. Coombs, the first director of the International Institute for Educational Planning in Paris, developed the general principles which he thought ought to guide educational planning. I reproduce them here amplified by the viewpoints I have snapped up in the course of attending conferences at the institute.

(1) Educational planning must be integrated with social and economic planning in general. It must both socially and temporally be comprehensive. It cannot be restricted to the society which exists today. Having regard to the long 'production cycle' that characterizes the educational system, it should preferably look at least twenty years ahead. Much of past planning has been done in 'bits and pieces'; an example is the five-year plan that seeks to realize basic education for all children or to build a specified number of new universities by the end of that time. Such plans knock many balances askew. Physical

plant has often been lacking, not to mention manpower, mostly teachers. Just as often the established objectives have not been matched by money in the state treasury. The result in many developing countries – and in the developed too for that matter – has been a quantitative expansion of the school at the price of lowered quality. Nor have the advanced countries escaped these problems.

Another imbalance has to do with the educational system's ability to give the job world what it needs. The courses taught should be such as to obviate the risk of turning out too much manpower with certain skills into a labour market that wants other manpower, such as technicians, and can't get enough of it. Many developing countries, in their eagerness to have education help them catch up with their former colonial masters, have tended to imitate uncritically what these left behind them in the way of an educational system. The result, as can be seen in Africa, has been to produce a surplus of manpower for white collar occupations of the kind that urbanized countries need in large quantities, whereas the school has done pitifully little to improve the dominant sector of the economy, namely agriculture, which for these countries is likely to be a matter of life and death for a long time to come.

The main problem facing planners is not to extend education in terms of enrolments and number of years of formal schooling, but to realize the social and economic problems that a given country will face during the foreseeable future. Among other things, this means affecting structure and quality in such a way that more can be accomplished within the limits dictated by available resources.

On the other hand, and this is particularly true for the advanced countries, educational planning must not be distorted by exclusive concern with the manpower approach. As we said earlier, education is also consumption, the nurture of human beings without ulterior pragmatic motives. It is therefore quite in order to plan for an 'overcapacity', subject only to what finances permit. People are educated and trained for more than mere breadwinning.

The requirement that educational planning be co-ordinated with other economic and social planning embodies the growing insight that the educational system is no longer an island by itself within society, but is closely intertwined with its other sectors.

(2) The educational system must be seen as a whole, which among other things means planning for all levels *at the same time*. If, as has often happened, the primary level is planned first, the planner will risk frustration for having neglected the secondary and the university level. To build up the primary school, teachers must be trained, and for that purpose there must be people who train the teachers. In other words, steps taken at the primary level imply steps at the other levels. That explains why the lack of an overall planning in the educational system has often led to bottlenecks. And the most common bottleneck has been the shortage of qualified teachers.

(3) Qualitative planning is every bit as important as the quantitative. A planner who disregards the qualitative aspects is liable to extrapolate today's *status quo* as regards school organization, types of instruction and other parameters into the future. The school's 'methods of production' must be reformed in the light of modern technical resources available to us and with due regard to the shortage of highly qualified people that applies both to developing and advanced countries. Today's school is just as much in need of a technological transformation as agriculture was in Europe several decades ago.

To many, the very mention of educational planning is anathema. In the United States it conjures up spectres of socialism. Among the less prejudiced it evokes associations with regimentation and curtailed freedom. But planning can in principle be combined with a considerable degree of freedom, especially if it is carried out while there is still scope for choosing priorities. The failure to plan in time against, say, air and water pollution, so that it can be kept within reasonable bounds if not avoided, curtails the freedom of those who have to inhabit a given area in the future. Actually, planning in the modern society, by contrast with the *laissez-faire* of an earlier day, *creates* freedom in the long run.

The need for systems approaches in applied social science

Everyone knows that our high standard of living builds upon a sophisticated technology, which in turn rests on advances in the natural sciences. These are usually applied in 'fragmented' form. To cope with a widespread disease, for example, the researchers first try to explore its etiology as a guide for developing a cure. They look for better roads and bridges in order to improve communication and therefore attempt to develop better construction materials. To suppress or extirpate the organisms that threaten our cultivated plants, they investigate suitable biocides. A common element of these 'fragmented' measures is that they are usually carried out with a short or narrow perspective. That is why many productive gains and improvements in standard of living have seriously upset the equilibrium of the ecosystem. The improved standard has been bought at a price that may inflict disaster on the next generation. Air and water pollution is a consequence of this technology. Given the rate at which we are now consuming the earth's resources of fossil fuels, the atmosphere may well have enough carbon dioxide in another three or four decades to start melting the polar icecaps and raise sea levels throughout the world.

Much more could be said about the price we are paying

for the comforts that derive from the despoliation of nature. In the following paragraphs, however, we shall be concerned with what social scientists can do to espouse 'systems approaches' to avoid and – not least – prevent the consequences of technological advance. The perils posed by fragmented expertise are all the greater the more specialized that research, both basic and applied, becomes. The 'linear' causal thinking prevailing particularly in the natural sciences has promoted the tendency for everyone to study his own tiny segment of an interconnected and complicated reality.

In Sweden, the past few decades have witnessed the adoption of far-reaching reforms in social welfare and education. The decisions of parliament and government are spelled out in laws and regulations, and their implementation is vested in different administrative agencies. These bodies take pains to nourish their activities so as to foster their own growth. Even though exceptions can be cited, most authorities anxiously protect their respective purviews, which means that joint consultations often have no more than a platonic character.

However, the greater number of major public issues cut across administrative and scientific borderlines. But precisely because of the inability, or even refusal, to realize that the big issues are 'systems problems', whose solution requires the co-ordinated efforts of several administrative agencies and teams of experts, the essentials of 'major reforms' sometimes never leave the paper on which they are written.

To my mind, the most flagrant international example of a non-systems approach is the 'War on Poverty' declared by the Johnson administration in the US. Here poverty has been fought piecemeal by widely disparate federal agencies. Thus huge sums have been spent on the Head Start programme to give pre-school children from underprivileged homes stimulating and individualized experiences before they attend regular school. But as evaluation of the programme has also shown, a paltry few hours of such contact for slum children has little or no effect unless large-scale and vigorous action is simultaneously taken to deal with the other causes of cultural poverty, such as unemployment and wretched housing. Indeed, the programme makes a good object lesson for the thesis I have been preaching, namely that educational reforms cannot serve as substitutes for social reforms. The latter must be co-ordinated, and they must also partly precede the former.

As a Swedish example of a situation where a systems approach is badly needed, we can take juvenile delinquency. Several studies have shown that preventive measures in this field require co-ordinated efforts by many agents: the police, the schools, the welfare services, the local business community, etc. Up to now there has been a striking lack of co-ordinated effort by the educational and welfare establishments – to mention just one example, since many other examples of watertight compartments could be cited. Perhaps their consequences are most fraught in city planning and nature conservation.

What is needed at the policymaking level is a group of broadly oriented social scientists who are willing to take a cross-disciplinary look at the issues. These people should develop the systems approaches that must precede the co-ordination of measures which produces suitable strategies for the treatment of problems. So far only the military has run central co-ordinating bodies of this type. In many countries the defence staff is not primarily an administrative agency, but an organization for 'forward' thinking on problems of military strategy and tactics. We would also need co-ordinating bodies in the fields of social welfare and city planning.

It may be objected that efforts at co-ordinated planning and implementation are in fact made through such media as conferences and seminars. But it is not enough to have experts from different fields convene for a few days in an auditorium, where everyone reads a neat paper on his aspect of a big problem complex, e.g., road safety or juvenile delinquency. We need a number of persons who, unhampered by daily routines in an administrative agency, can permanently explore their way towards 'systems solutions', preferably in frequent touch with the men who formulate policy. Many central agencies have their scientific advisers, but their contributions are as fragmented as the agencies themselves: the information they give mainly reflects their special domains of competence.

Obviously, systems approaches should apply to both the planning and execution stages. Here I chiefly have in mind the efforts of social scientists — for two reasons: first, because up to now they have taken so little part in the planning that relates to the community at large; and second, because they now have a vital mission to perform in trying to restore the balance between man and nature that technology has upset with such grave consequences. But it is also obvious that natural scientists, technicians and social scientists must join forces to tackle the big environmental problems such as pollution and the preservation of natural amenities. For this purpose it is necessary not only to devise technical solutions (actually, many of these have been put forward already), but also to prevail on people to accept the costs or sacrifices which these solutions require.

In the final analysis, the fragmentation to get rid of first is the one that has evolved from the encyclopedic philosophy of school education. Ecological thinking in science makes a good start. However, the fixed disciplines as such must be broken up regardless of how strongly entrenched they are. A problem-centred approach to teaching can provide the perspective and the overview which will make a systems thinker of every citizen.

5 Education towards the year 2000

Some assumptions about the 'learning society'

Educators who conjecture imaginatively about the future
of the institutions they deal with are supposed to start
from a number of reasonable assumptions about the
matrix of tomorrow's society. But as we shall see presently,
some of these assumptions can be regarded as highly
reasonable, while others must be looked upon as dubious
and even highly controversial. The margins of uncertainty
which govern here are not least determined by unforeseen
technological innovations, irrespective of whether these
are regarded as advances or calamities. My attempts in the
following pages to outline what the educational system
will look like by the end of this century should be viewed
as a preliminary exercise for a research project which,
equipped with a broader array of data, more powerful
analytical tools and stricter theoretical considerations,
seeks to construct a model of the future educational
system. The language of Swedish official investigations has
begun to employ the term 'illustrative exercise'
(*räkneexempel*). On the basis of certain assumptions such
things as student enrolment are calculated. The term could

well apply to this paper, which to all intents and purposes
has a pedagogical aim, namely to illustrate what research
into the future is all about. I shall begin by making certain
assumptions about future society, and in so doing separate
assumptions about the community at large from those
which pertain to working life. The consequences for
education will then be drawn from these assumptions.
However, the attempts to form a picture of tomorrow's
school must also be based on assumptions relating to
society and the educational system at large. Some of
these assumptions have already been discussed in a
preliminary way on pp. 197–202.

Accelerating change

In the decades to come we shall have to reckon with an
accelerated process of change in many respects. That will
apply with particular force to the economy, where rates of
growth in the highly industrialized countries have so far
increased. This growth will be accompanied by a rise in
individual standards of living. Applications of electronics
and computer technology by private enterprise and public
administration have triggered off a second industrial
revolution. A problem common to both developing and
industrialized countries is the 'culture lag' not only of
institutions (as in the educational system) but also of
attitudes and values. They derive from a state of society
where the external determinants of technology, economics
and institutions were different. An example is the impact
that the introduction of the contraceptive pill may be
expected to have on existing sexual morality. Indeed, the
rapid changes wrought by technology in working and living
conditions cannot avoid generating cultural maladjustment
or even neurotic reactions. For the majority of individuals,
great strains are imposed by new techniques, new material
conditions of human existence and new interpersonal
relations. The new technology will require many people

not only to continue and supplement their previous education, but even to undergo actual retraining because occupational experience and skills may quickly become obsolete. Changes of occupation or job will entail great geographic mobility. New sections of the community, embracing different kinds of technicians and experts, will become more influential whereas others, such as those consisting of the owners of business enterprises, will have their power diminished in relative terms. The climate of pluralistic values will be hard on the many people who want clear-cut guidelines for their judgements and actions. The risk of maladjusted reactions as embodied in fascist ideology, or in the search for scapegoats to expiate the sins of this world, will probably intensify, the greater the discrepancy between technology and value patterns becomes.

Urbanization will continue at an accelerated pace. More and more people will accordingly be living in cities and towns, with all that this implies in the way of informal contacts and confrontation between people having different backgrounds both of upbringing and values. Social controls are weaker and contacts between generations fewer in the urbanized environment than in the countryside or village where everyone knows his neighbour and the individual is far more 'visible' than in the anonymous fabric of the city. Reduced social controls tend to aggravate criminal behaviour, especially among teenagers. In recent years the informal contacts in large enterprises and organizations have made the so-called alienation problem more pronounced than before. In relation to the larger, imponderable whole, the individual finds it difficult to view his own contribution in perspective and indeed to define his own identity. Under such circumstances, it lies ready to hand for fascist and other theories of salvation to make capital of the collective reactions of maladjustment.

Family and leisure

The family as an institution has been very much transformed in industrialized and urbanized society. What has happened is essentially the following: families have become smaller and more seldom house three generations under the same roof. On average, parents have fewer children than in the past. The family performs fewer common functions. Families of yesteryear which tilled the soil or pursued a craft were frequently real communities of both work and leisure. Today's livelihoods are earned outside the home, and not only by the paterfamilias. The mothers of more than half today's urban families do the same, either full-time or part-time. Their children stay longer and longer in school, and it is becoming increasingly common to have different kinds of institutions look after them before they start regular school. By and large this transformation may be said to have left the family with two functions: reproduction of the human species and socialization of very small children. The two other main functions, i.e. the economic and the protective, have been increasingly assumed by the community at large.

On the other hand the increments to leisure in the wake of shorter working hours outside the home and of longer weekends point in the direction of greatly enlarged 'co-operation in amusement and play'. The weekend cottage, the car and the joint pursuit of hobbies combine to give the family a growing body of shared experiences. During the next few decades the advance in living standards which economic growth permits will confront families with the choice of increasing either their consumption or their leisure. Inside the home, too, leisure has been enhanced by all sorts of technical improvements or time savers. At the same time the question of how leisure can be employed towards better self-realization, the creation of sensible time fillers, has taken on greater urgency. Owing to longer life expectancy, and the tendency to concentrate childbearing into the early years of marriage, a growing proportion of wives will have other roles to perform than keeping house and raising children. A higher incidence of divorce is also likely, at the same time as marriage, considered as a formal contract for cohabitation, loses its importance in consequence of modern contraceptive techniques.

It has been emphasized that the penchant of contemporary society for moulding 'organization men', i.e. people who present the appearance of being well-adjusted, conformist, faceless and effective workers in the firm, organization or 'movement', will impart greater strength to the family as an emotional anchorage. Because of increasing geographic mobility and because contacts with most people outside the home are bound to be superficial, and above all ephemeral, marriage provides a facility for emotional ties and role identity that other social groups cannot offer. A corollary of this observation is that the organized society and its institutions, big enterprises, the proliferating public authorities, the school etc., will become more and more impersonal and will be less and less disposed to permit the individual to 'let off steam'. In the majority of cases, critical and aggressive reactions will be directly punished by withdrawal of benefits and subtle discourtesies. The family can then become the place where frustrations and anxiety will find a more uninhibited outlet. In a world otherwise characterized by casual and impersonal relations, the family will thus become a forum for the sharing of emotions and the partaking of intimate solidarity. The consequence for marriage in a formalized world will be to make it more of an institution for establishing identity and promoting individual and genuine modes of expression. It will counterbalance organized life and in that way become a 'rehabilitative institution which generates new "coping power" ' (Pauline Wahlen).

Raising children will be a mission that fosters individuality, where the establishment of emotional identifications will have the utmost importance.

Mass communication

Mass media and growing geographic mobility will increase communications not only within countries but also between them. To an overwhelming extent, the world of the year 2000 will be a world of internationalism. Advances in the developing countries towards controlling the population explosion will permit a rise in living standards and educational levels. During the next two decades the task of coping with poverty and famine, which is now the lot of most people on this earth, will become a main task of the industrialized countries. Broadened international communication will make the masses of Asia, Africa and Latin America increasingly conscious of the gaps in living standards, which in turn will give rise to social revolutionary movements. On the whole it is likely that the rapid adoption of Western technology by developing countries will afflict them with problems of cultural adjustment and social change greater than those experienced in the Western industrial countries.

Communication satellites can make an increasing number of people more vividly aware of world events than ever before. This will give greater urgency to the problem of imparting a representative character to reality in mass media generally, and television in particular. More and more of the reality to which people react in the mass communication society is the reality which mass media convey, and less and less that which they themselves directly observe. An event that is not covered by mass media tends to be one that simply does not exist. From this it follows that the determination of what shall be communicated, for example over television, must essentially rest with the community at large and not with commercial interests. The risk of excluding controversial issues and minority opinions is considerably greater in a commercially controlled mass medium than in one which represents different sections of the community.

The tourist industry owes its explosive growth in the affluent industrial countries to the diffusion of opportunities for large masses to travel, not least to other countries. Higher standards of consumption have been accompanied by a vigorously expanding advertising industry, where brand-name advertising has become an increasingly conspicuous feature. Whether he is buying capital goods or consumer goods, the individual is confronted with a growingly dissonant chorus of public relations men.

Health problems

Improved standards of material well-being have been achieved by technology at the price of serious health problems. The waste products of our technical civilization are in the process of destroying water and air. Ruthless exploitation of natural resources in many places will impoverish coming generations unless restrictive measures are taken promptly. The enormous despoliation of nature inflicted by water contaminants has the undesired side effect of curtailing recreational opportunities. Already by the mid-1960s air pollution was responsible for the smoggy atmosphere of many metropolitan areas. The proliferation of gasoline-powered motor vehicles aggravates the problem, which is further compounded by many types of industrial activity. It may be assumed that technicians and urban planners will soon be much more aware of the litter problems and health hazards posed by technology, and hence more willing than the present generation to deal with them effectively.

The very style of life in modern society engenders health problems of its own. As if activities requiring the exertion of muscle and sinew were not diminishing anyway, there will be even less need of it as industrial engineering continues to reduce the component of manual labour. The ever growing preference for locomotion by vehicle, especially by private car, makes greater the risk of obesity. Higher standards of living will also be reflected in a tendency to overeat. The stepped-up tempo of life and the diverse causes of frustration associated with a more complex and rigidly bureaucratized society will make cardiosvascular diseases increasingly common, with over-eating as a contributory cause. A task of growing importance for the community at large will be to sponsor programmes of health education both during and after the schoolgoing period. By virtue of medical advances, which will surely also overcome the cardiovascular diseases in due course, average longevity will increase even more. This fact of itself, together with a trend towards individually selected retirement age, will enable an ever larger proportion of people to reach an age which makes it necessary to find meaningful pursuits even after the termination of regular careers.

Bureaucratization

As observed earlier, an ever deeper impress is being stamped on society by the large units, the big organizations, within both the private and the public sector. We are rushing headlong into an *organization society*. Public agencies of government and administration will continue to expand, a consequence not only of the need for better planning, co-ordination and control of such activity in the increasingly complex society which its organs have decided upon, but also of the tendency towards 'empire-building' inherent in the bureaucratic system itself. The bureaucrats will become more important persons because they tend to become more identified with 'their' agency and represent them vis-à-vis their clients. This also holds true for the administrative hierarchies of private firms and the agents of unions and professional associations. The individual will increasingly perceive himself to be a lost Kafka figure in this mighty and hard-to-fathom apparatus. An overshadowing social problem for the year 2000, and hence an important political problem, will have to do with how the individual is to escape from being 'alienated' in a mass society, and with how he shall be protected against injustices committed by bureaucrats in government agencies and private firms. It seems likely that efforts will be made at workplaces and within organizations to create a counterpart to the emotional anchorage that the family provides. Viewpoints and reactions emanating from the 'grass roots' have proved notoriously unamenable to canalization through the formal hierarchy which characterizes the linear organization of firms and government agencies. The 'grass roots' can make their case better heard and more easily relayed to the top echelons by means of small informal discussion groups, as well as by staff organizations consisting of 'fiduciaries'. On the whole, and this will be particularly true for a small country like Sweden, the purport of growing industrial democracy will be to give employees a greater say in the decision-making counsels and also a larger share of the profits. The process of abolishing private ownership initiated by tax legislation will thereby be continued and eventually concluded.

The learning society

Society toward the year 2000 will confer status decreasingly on the basis of social background or, assuming there is any left, inherited wealth. To a growing extent, *educated ability* will be democracy's replacement for passed-on social prerogatives. The technician, the expert or the scientist will be a more important person not only on the strength of his know-how and proficiency in planning, but also because the information he gives to policymakers will be so complicated that the latter will increasingly tend to waive their authority. As is pointed out below, the question of expertise versus the 'common sense' of ordinary people boils down to weighing the relative merits of general education and special training. Future society is likely to be more 'meritocratic' in the sense that ability and education will matter more for social upgrading than in the past.

Among all the 'explosions' that have come into use as labels to describe rapidly changing Western society, the term 'knowledge explosion' is one of the most appropriate. Reference is often made to the 'knowledge industry' (Fritz Machlup), meaning both the producers of knowledge, such as the research institutes, and its distributors, e.g. schools, mass media, book publishers, libraries and so on. What we have been witnessing since the mid-1960s in the field of distribution technology may well have begun to revolutionize the communication of knowledge within another ten years or so. I have in mind here the marriage between 'hardware' and 'software', on the one side of which are the computer manufacturers (e.g. IBM) and the reprographic industry (e.g. Xerox), and on the other side publishers of books, newspapers and periodicals. That which looms on the horizon is the possibility of communicating both visual and verbal information to individual terminals, installed either in classrooms or in homes. Learning transmitted in this way can be controlled by information-producing programmes which are stored in computer memory units or otherwise kept in some central facility where it is accessible in the form which suits the individual. To the same extent that information quickly becomes available, especially if it has high value in terms of durability and application range, it will be necessary to examine subject matter presented at school much more thoroughly than now with reference to what has to be memorized or not.

The passage of another two decades ought to see near total realization of the principle of *equal opportunities* for all to receive as much education as they are thought capable of absorbing. Economic and geographic barriers will be virtually dismantled. The lagging attitudes in different social strata, namely that to receive a certain type of education is either 'proper' or 'improper', will have diminished to vanishing point. In many countries on both sides of the Atlantic, parents of the children who start school in the 1980s will themselves have grown up when universal secondary schooling was being prepared or implemented. They will have high aspirations for the education of their children, higher than they themselves achieved even though a high proportion of them will have qualified for university entrance. Beginning in 1980 it is likely that in several highly industrialized countries like the United States, Japan and Sweden, at least 80 per cent of an age cohort will pursue an education (though not necessarily in school) up to the age of nineteen or twenty. The only limits on personal aspirations will be those imposed by allocation of the national resources. The result will be that the higher seats of learning in which a majority of young people around the age of twenty are enrolled, including the institutions which give basic university degrees, will become centres of culture in a quite different way from before. Sheer numbers will turn these undergraduates into a power factor, whose significance will not be lost on the mass media and the consumption industries which aim at the youth market.

By comparison with earlier generations, the young people in tomorrow's learning society will be much more articulate. Equipped with broader horizons and greater awareness of world problems, and also because fewer of them will have had to 'work their way up' than their parents, they will be searching for other goals and other meanings to life than getting on in the world. In several so-called affluent countries young people are already rejecting the puritan ethic — of the hardworking man — under whose auspices their parents 'made it'. This means that the gap between generations will widen, in any event the gap which relates to values as to what is socially desirable. In consequence of the 'youth revolt' young people will demand — and get — increased influence. The prevailing tendency up to the 1960s was that which characterized middle class upbringing and middle class education in the Western world, namely that until young persons finished their education they were to be treated like incompetent, immature children, to be denied all authority, for example, over school affairs. The lack of 'functional participation' in actual school work, with the consequences this has had in the form of unforthcoming social maturity and the tendency to shift the pivot of social life to points outside the school, should by the late 1970s have led to another dispensation, whereby more students in both secondary and higher education will be in on the planning and decisions which bear on their studies.

The working community
The shift from manufacturing industry to service industry, which has been in full swing since the early 1950s, will tend to accelerate. One is no longer tied down as before to stationary jobs with relatively routine duties. In manufacturing industry the effect of continuing technical rationalization has been to substitute machinery for human muscle in more and more operations, at the same time as the production process itself increasingly comes under automatic controls with the adoption of modern electronic and data-processing methods. The blue collar worker of old will become a skilled technician who performs a general monitorial function. He will have to know how the 'machinery works' and be ready to take action if something

goes wrong, because the machinery entrusted to him will be incomparably more expensive than in the past.

The service industry will have a considerable part of its practitioners engaged in medical services and education. However, a great many people will also be working in other service sectors such as tourism and catering. Many services formerly provided by the home for itself will be supplied by outside organizations, such as food preparation, laundry, cleaning, transportation, etc. This will effect a change in the knowledge and skills required by the working community. The service industry will set particularly great store by communication and flexibility. A premium will be put on the ability to communicate with customers orally and in writing, to deal with them smoothly and easily, and make the best of their wishes and complaints. For these purposes it will not be enough to master the native tongue; familiarity with one or more foreign languages will become increasingly essential.

An important consequence of modern technology and greater efficiency in manufacturing industry will be to professionalize more of the duties performed by employees. The fewer the routine and repetitive operations that are required of an employee, the more he will have need of general education and specialized occupational experience. Technological advances, not least those identified with electronics, will definitely not 'enslave' individuals to the machine. On the contrary, the machine will take over the simpler tasks, leaving the worker to deal with more sophisticated tasks, those which require an intelligent overview and a flexible choice of alternatives.

Having regard to the speedy transformation of the economic system, fixed commitment to any one line of vocational training will increasingly become a dubious proposition. So rapid is the process of change in major sectors that a person who has gone to great lengths to master the intricacies of his particular craft cannot be sure whether his skills will be marketable only a few years hence. From this two consequences follow. First, skills of the kind which involve the ability to listen, speak, read, write and count, and also the ability on his own to find adequate knowledge, will take on ever greater importance. Second, it will also be important to have a command of certain fundamentals in different subject areas, i.e. familiarity with the concepts, principles and methods which constitute these subjects as disciplines, as fields of human learning. It will be necessary to assimilate a body of *general education*, large enough to cover the broad unforeseen spectrum of tasks that will be confronted both in the working community and outside it. The normal course of a life career will probably have to make *recurring* provision for further education and in some cases for retraining as well in order to prepare for a completely different occupational sector. It has been observed that the specialized knowledge which an engineer learned as part of his education in the mid-1950s found but moderate application in his sphere of activities ten years later. But in so far as he had acquired a good basic education in science and a good general orientation in technology, he could familiarize himself with the new without too much trouble.

By the 1980s it should be the rule rather than the exception for a working career to be dramatically affected by a technology which translates human talent into machinery, information systems, computer programmes and 'precooked' knowledge which is immediately retrievable for use. Lifelong education, at least in those occupations of a more professional nature, looks like becoming a normal fact of life.

The working community of the end of the century will very likely be characterized not only by full employment but also by a guaranteed minimum income, or in the event of disability or unused working capacity by a 'negative tax', i.e. contributions out of public funds. As mentioned earlier, industrial democracy will probably have developed to the point where employees have a greater say in decisions affecting production. Ownership rights will become an even foggier concept and to that extent a matter of secondary interest for employees.

The educational system towards the year 2000

Quantitative growth. The sweeping portrayal of a changing society given above has sought to provide a general background for the assumptions stated below as to how the educational system will look a few decades from now.

Two developments may be taken for granted: enrolments in higher education will continue to expand, and more years will be devoted to systematic learning. More than anything else we can feel sure of a spectacular quantitative growth in the educational system in terms of pupils and students and the number of years they will be spending in the system. Adult education (or continuing education as it is sometimes labelled) will probably expand more than youth education.

To take Sweden as an example: the period beginning with 1950 has been marked by an 'enrolment explosion', which has visited its rolling impact upon elementary, secondary and university levels in turn. Elementary education in the nine-year comprehensive school had become almost fully implemented by the time the 1960s had run their course. Differentiation by streams, about which there has been so much discussion since the late 1940s, will soon belong to past history, having been limited to grade 9 by virtue of parliamentary decision in 1962 and since then abolished in practice even there after curriculum revision. The strong tendency towards academic choice or 'academic lopsidedness' which has impinged on the next age stage, embracing the 16–19 year olds, has

served to move the differentiation problem one rung
higher up the age ladder. Reports from committees,
submissions and parliamentary papers abound in
utterances on the establishment of an integrated
gymnasium (i.e. where the pre-university school, vocational
school and continuation school are combined). In the
prolongation of current trends one can dimly see the
makings of a comprehensive school serving young people
up to the age of eighteen, i.e. a situation resembling that
which obtains in the more economically developed states
of the US. The economy's manpower needs, as well as the
heightened demands for educational consumption which
follow from improved living standards, will mean that
nearly half the youth population will want education at the
post-secondary level. Even the universities will probably
'burst at the seams', which in turn looks like ushering in
two types of institution: the one mainly concerned with
preparing for vocations on the basis of a first degree, and
the other with the training of researchers at doctoral and
post-doctoral level.

Economic consequences. Given a development such as
this in a country such as Sweden, where almost all
education is paid for out of public funds and where even
public subsidies are forthcoming to compensate young
people for some of the income they do not earn by staying
longer in school, severe strains are inevitably imposed on
government finances and ultimately on national resources.
All the ardent talk of rationalization and the desire to have
the work of educational research and development aim at
manpower economics in schools should, of course, be
seen in this light. The heaviest expense of running an
educational system is incurred by the teacher, and major
savings stand to be gained by the more efficient
deployment of this manpower. Opportunities will be
opened up for more admissions to those schools which

have had to limit their enrolments for financial reasons. For some time it will presumably be realistic to expect that priority will be given to quantity (the number of educational opportunities) ahead of quality (the average level of accomplishment among the educated).

It seems safe to assume that the future school system will bear institutional features that will be at great variance with past tradition in many respects. The buildings which now go under the name of schools and run up a big construction bill, not to mention the rapidly increasing expense of equipping them, will surely have to be put to more effective, particularly more continuous, use in the future. Far from looking as schools have always looked, they will take on more of the guise of community centres or learning centres, where children, young people and adults will meet not only for instruction, lectures and study groups, but also for a broad array of other cultural activities, such as performances of plays, concerts, discussions, and leisure and hobby pursuits.

The costs of education embrace not only the direct outlays, those expended on the educational plant itself, but also the indirect loss of production and income which results from opting for education instead of gainful employment. Even though the question of whether or not lost income ought to be counted as an educational cost is open to debate, it cannot be denied that education would be easier to bear in the macroeconomic short term if the young people were out working part of the time rather than going to school. This argument acquires added weight at a time when the numbers of young people pursuing a full-time education are growing with explosive speed. Nor can it be denied that a large slice of education is not an investment but quite simply consumption, something which we in Sweden have regarded as not only legitimate but also self-evident. The Soviet Union, no doubt motivated by compelling grounds of social and economic cost, has gone in for various educational models, which all have in common the aim to integrate education and productive work for people in their late teens. These young people spend certain days in factories and other days in classrooms. Longer periods of education sometimes alternate with longer periods of employment. The Russians have also committed themselves heavily to adult education, whose night classes are often attended or individual correspondence studies pursued after a full day on the job.

Spreading out the educational period. It is now possible to envisage a different balance between basic general education, vocational training and continuing education (retraining) than the one now struck. Tradition holds that as much education as possible ought to be squeezed into the early years of life. School should preferably be started at the earliest possible age. In the United States, a debate has been waged during the 1960s about what might be gained from letting 3–4 year olds learn to read and possibly write.

One can imagine a scheme to provide every citizen with a certain number of 'educational vouchers' which would guarantee free education after compulsory schooling for a specified length of time. It would then be up to the individual to decide whether he wanted to use up all his bonds at one go or spread them out. For example, some youngsters might be 'fed up' with school at the age of sixteen and prefer to leave even though their parents want them to continue. Knowing that further education is guaranteed for them, they could take jobs to gain the maturity and experience that would make a return to school more meaningful. Considerable savings could no doubt be made from putting off the completion of schooling till long past the age of twenty. Adults are admittedly much more expensive to educate per unit of time because their on-the-job inputs are more productive, but it should be reckoned that they would be able, with considerably less guidance and in a much shorter time, to assimilate knowledge and skills that often have to be pressed upon unmotivated young people, and with a lot of time wasted in the process. Adults have better motivation, are better able to see the relevance of what they learn, can plan better and can work to a much greater extent on their own without supervision.

No pretensions are made here to portray even the general outlines of a future educational system that is not solely cast in a school-type mould and does not rest on a time-honoured school organization. The best that can be done is to give indications and make observations about development trends which may be strengthened or weakened at some future time. As I have already pointed out, one can envisage an abandonment of the formal division between education in schools for children and young people on the one hand, and productive inputs in the economy on the other, inasmuch as education can be divided in time along different lines from those which now hold. The advent of institutionalized adult education administered by the local educational authorities in Sweden (not to be confused with the longstanding programmes of education for adults on a more informal basis run by the popular movements, such as the workers' movement or the temperance movement) has demonstrated that the old school-versus-work dichotomy is ripe for revision. And as has also been noted above, it is not necessary to devote full time to either education or work. A certain part of the day, or specified days in succession, may come to be spent in that institution called the school, whereas other times of the day or other full days can be given over to endeavour either in education or in productive work (indeed, the two activities may well become indistinguishable) in companies, etc.

Future channels of education. What are the institutions that will be rendering contributions to tomorrow's educational system?

It stands to reason that the school in its traditional sense will continue to play the dominant role. However, the uses to which it is put will take in *all* ages and its manpower resources will include not only teachers as conventionally defined but also experts from various walks of life: capable exponents of different professions, officials and politicians. Boarding schools and camp schools would appear to be likely variants. We already have in-residence education for young people with special handicaps or for those looked after in corrective schools. Considering that it will be cheaper for society to give young people who are born in homes where they risk serious maladjustment an in-residence schooling in place of social therapy induced by delinquency or other antisocial behaviour, the establishment of more such schools must be taken into account. The other variant, camp school, enables teachers and pupils to be together in short-term classes where educative contacts in the broadest sense can be established and strengthened.

Alongside the institutional school we have the new era's leading agents of cultural influence: the mass media. These will be increasingly incorporated in the actual schoolteaching. Before long it is likely that the average pupil at home will listen to the radio or watch television for at least as long as he watches and listens to a teacher in school.

In certain countries, such as Australia and the Soviet Union, correspondence courses have had great importance for the instruction of young people, but they are also important for adult education, as in Sweden. Its potential will increase to the same extent that instruction by computer is introduced and methods for the marking and individualization of special exercises in this instruction are worked out.

Up to now the educational associations connected with the people's movements in Sweden have exclusively confined their activities to adult education. Indeed, they have even tended to shy away from that term, preferring to designate their work as 'informal, free popular education', which has not primarily aimed at providing bread-and-butter knowledge and economically measurable results but rather 'pure' general education. But in that respect the main achievement, perhaps, is that a reassessment has taken place guided by an increased insight into the social realities.

The educational associations nurture a major pedagogical tradition, mainly centred on the methodology of so-called study circles. Learning, of course, always involves self-activity, but it is the study circles that have developed self-activity into an art after decades of experience, which they do by stimulating the motivation of participants and emphasizing co-operation with the purpose of achieving social maturity. If nothing else, the teaching of civics in school could certainly draw on this experience capital if greater provision were made to have representatives of educational associations teach this subject, or in any case come in as 'resource persons'.

In small countries, where fluency in one of the world languages is an imperative and some command of one or two others highly desirable, much of the school's time schedule goes to foreign languages. Experiments have lately been undertaken at the secondary level to locate some of this instruction in the country whose language the pupil is supposed to learn. With increasing communications in our day and age, there is every likelihood that external courses will become a common feature of the educational system, with provision made not only for languages but also for other subjects, both to be studied as part of regularly allotted longer stays abroad.

In spite of the considerably greater interest taken by the

business community in Europe since the early 1950s in matters relating to education and schools – in certain countries, for example West Germany, businessmen actually spearhead the drive for necessary school reforms – there is still a big, and to some extent necessary, gap between the type of education given in the classroom and that which may later become appropriate at the workplace. So as to impart to young people a broader experience of 'functional participation' and to stimulate their motivation by making them feel the relevance of what they are doing, it ought to be a matter of top priority to investigate all the educational (in both the material and formal senses of this term) possibilities which can lie in business-sponsored programmes of in-company training. It is likely that the development set in train by the experimental work in Sweden in the early 1950s, when certain categories of young people were enabled through work experience to receive for a few weeks practical vocational guidance on the premises of firms (a programme that was later extended to all young people) will be further accentuated, so that more teenagers who so desire can take their education in 'sandwich' form, spending certain times in school, other times in a company.

Work practices in the end-of-the-century school. Perhaps the most dominant feature of the end-of-the-century school we can imagine will have to do with the change in work practices. The acquisition of knowledge will probably present a quite different picture in certain fundamental respects.

(1) The emphasis will be put on learning, not on teaching. Hitherto the school has operated on the theory that learning necessarily presupposes teaching. But with the growing realization that these activities are not identical, and that teaching may in extreme cases even impede productive learning, the direction of focus has been on

economic management of the teaching function, as manifested by close analysis of its real import and the purposes it is supposed to serve. An essential consideration of the teacher's duties, of course, is to deploy his working time most effectively.

(2) Labour-saving facilities will make their way into the school to a greater extent. These facilities will embrace both 'hardware' and 'software': in the former category, appliances such as projectors, tape recorders and learning machines; in the latter, printed material such as exercise booklets, work cards and programmed textbooks. The school has long been unresponsive to the technological revolution that has reduced humdrum chores and raised production in industry.

(3) Although the main educational emphasis will have shifted from content subjects, such as history and geography, to skill subjects, such as the mother tongue and mathematics, this will in no way diminish the quantum of knowledge required. Towards this end great emphasis will have been put on teaching pupils how to acquire knowledge by themselves, which in turn will demand more initiative and self-activity on their part.

(4) A new organization of work has begun to make its entry with the abolition of the breakdown (for all subjects) by grades, with provision for flexible class sizes depending on the mode of instruction used (one-way communication, discussion, independent work).

What are the modes of instruction that may be assumed to hold sway in tomorrow's school? Having considered this matter at greater length in another context, I shall confine myself here to a brief summary.

To begin with, we are already heading towards a new physical organization of work which signifies that the division of pupils by grades has lost importance, that the size of the group taught is determined by the mode of instruction and that the pupil is more likely to face several teachers rather than a single teacher or instructor in any one subject. The division of pupils by grades, largely coinciding with age levels and entailing upward movement once a year in all subjects, contravenes what has long been common knowledge in differential psychology. Considerable variability in age-homogeneous classes already begins to emerge in the first grade, and the variability increases throughout the schooling period by and large irrespective of non-promotions and assignments to special classes. Individual differences in scholastic ability cannot account for more than half the variability in scholastic achievement that exists between pupils. In the future, therefore, consideration must be given to grouping the pupils in a way that eliminates grade division and the kind of differentiation by streams that freezes individual choice of studies and occupations later on.

Further, we have taken the first groping steps towards an organization of work where the size of a class is determined by what takes place there. If the communication is mostly of the one-way kind, such as a film showing or lecture, more than 100 pupils can constitute the class. If it takes the form of intensive teacher-led instruction involving interaction between teacher and pupils, as well as between pupils, the group should not consist of more than ten to twelve pupils. Analyses carried out in several countries show that the teacher in an average class spends at least half his time talking, demonstrating, screening films, administering or monitoring tests, or engaging in similar tasks for whose performance class size within reasonable limits is irrelevant. The large group may be said to have three main functions: to motivate pupils, to introduce subject matter and exercises, and to report on exercises performed by individual pupils. The purpose of working in small groups is to afford the opportunity for common treatment of subject matter, to train analytical skills, and to develop the give and take of argumentative discussion. It is therefore of central importance for socialization. The independent work chiefly relates to individual problem-solving and training in various skills, for example foreign languages. A third element of the work organization is so-called team teaching. The realization has dawned that there is little rationality in making *one* teacher responsible for all the instruction in one given subject or in all subjects that belong to a certain stage. The membership of a teaching team is understood to include not only the fully qualified head teacher and other teachers, but also assistants or helpers, who may be student teachers, clerks or housewives. It follows that a teaching team can permit a considerable differentiation of roles, for instance by enabling every member to render a personal contribution in that segment of a subject or with that methodology for which he or she is best fitted.

Perhaps the most sweeping transformation of work practices in the school which looms ahead is the development of more or less complete individualization, and upon this most of the teacher's endeavours will converge. The teacher will then be a person who diagnoses the status of every pupil, who sees to it that the pupil is confronted with appropriate subject matter and/or experiences (the latter taken to mean that all knowledge need not be verbally communicated) and who checks on individual progress. The occasions offered for such instruction must be such that each pupil is permitted to learn under optimal conditions. For this purpose a key role will be played by the new individualized facilities, as well as by the supplementary material entering into the 'prescriptions', partly based on computer-stored information, which the teacher writes out for the pupil for work in the school's 'mediatek' (book plus audiovisual library).

Bibliography[1]

Agrell, J. (1953) *Den nya skolan och försöksverksamheten.* (The new school on trial.) Uppsala: Lindblad.

Ahlström, K. G. (1967) Feedback functions in teaching machines. *Scandinavian Journal of Psychology,* 8, pp. 243–9.

Alkin, M. C. and Johnson, M. (1972) Some observations on educational research in Sweden. *Scandinavian Journal of Educational Research,* 16, pp. 2–3, 41–60.

Anderberg, R. *et al.* (1950) Redogörelser för det pedagogiska forskningsarbetet vid landets institutioner för psykologi och pedagogik. (Reports on research projects at the institutes of psychology and education.) *Skola och samhälle,* 31, pp. 193–240.

Andersson, B. E. (1969) *Studies in Adolescent Behaviour.* Stockholm: Almqvist & Wiksell.

Bjerstedt, Å. (1956) *Interpretation of Sociometric Choice Status.* Lund: Gleerup.

Bjerstedt, Å. (1956) *The Methodology of Preferential Sociometry: selected trends and some contributions.* New York: Beacon House.

[1] Relates mainly to the chapter on 'Two decades of educational research in Sweden', pp. 155–79.

Bjerstedt, Å. (1965) *Undervisningsprogrammering och urvärdering.* Stockholm: Scandinavian University Books.

Bjerstedt, Å. (1968) *Twelve Years of Educational and Psychological Research in Sweden.* Lund: Gleerup.

Boalt, G. (1947) *Skolutbildning och skolresultat för barn ur olika samhällsgrupper i Stockholm.* (School career and scholastic achievements of children from different social strata in Stockholm.) Stockholm: Norstedt.

Dahllöf, U. (1963) *Kraven på gymnasiet.* (Requirements on the gymnasium.) Stockholm: SOU: 22.

Dahllöf, U. (1967) *Skoldifferentiering och undervisningsförlopp.* (School differentiation and the teaching process.) Stockholm: Almqvist & Wiksell.

Dahllöf, U. (1971) *Ability Grouping, Content Validity and Curriculum Process Analysis.* New York: Teachers College Press.

Edfeldt, Å. (1959) *Silent Speech and Silent Reading.* Stockholm: Almqvist & Wiksell. (1967) *Educational Policy and Planning in Sweden.* Paris: OECD.

Ekman, G. (1951) Skolformer och begåvningsfördelning. (Distribution of ability within school types.) *Pedagogisk Tidskrift.* Nos. 1–2.

Elgqvist. I. (1965) Den ämnesteoretiska lärarutbildningen vid universiteten. In *Specialundersökn ngar om lärarutbildning.* Stockholm: SOU 1965: 31.

Elmgren, J. (1952) *School and Psychology.* Stockholm: Statens offentliga utredningar.

Halsey, A. H. (ed.) (1961) *Ability and Educational Opportunity.* Paris: OECD.

Henrysson, S. and Jansson, S. (1967) *Rekrytering till gymnasium och fackskola.* Stockholm: Report No. 25, School of Education.

Husén, T. (1949) Personalprüfungen bei der schwedischen Armee während des zweiten Weltkrieges. In *Progrès de*

la psychotechnique 1939–1945, pp. 280–91. Bern:
A. Francke AG.
Husén, T. (1950) *Rättstavningsförmågans psykologi. Några experimentella bidrag.* (The psychology of spelling: some experimental contributions.) Stockholm: Svensk Lärartidnings förlag.
Husén, T. (1950) Militärpsykologin i Sverige. (Military psychology in Sweden.) *Nordisk Psykologi*, 4, pp. 163–71.
Husén, T. (1951) The influence of schooling upon IQ. *Theoria*, 17, pp. 61–88.
Husén, T. (1962) Detection of ability and selection for educational purposes. In *The Yearbook of Education 1962*, pp. 295–314.
Husén, T. (1962a) *Problems of Differentiation in Swedish Compulsory Schooling.* Stockholm: Scandinavian University Books.
Husén, T. (1967) *International Study of Achievement in Mathematics*: Wiley. New York.
Husén, T. (1968a) Educational research and the state. In *Educational Research and Policy-making*, pp. 13–22. London: National Foundation for Educational Research in England and Wales.
Husén, T. (1968b) *Skola för 80–talet*. (Schools for the 1980s.) Stockholm: Almqvist & Wiksell.
Husén, T. (1969) *Talent, Opportunity and Career.* Stockholm: Almqvist & Wiksell.
Husén, T. (1971) *Education in the Year 2000*. Stockholm: National Board of Education.
Husén, T. (1972) *Social Background and Educational Career*. Paris: OECD.
Husén, T. (1973) *Svensk skola i internationell belysning: Naturorienterande ämnen.* (The Swedish school system in international perspective: science.) Stockholm: Almquist & Wicksell.

Husén, T. and Boalt, G. (1968) *Educational Research and Educational Change: the case of Sweden.* New York: Wiley.

Husén, T. and Dahllöf, U. (1965) Curriculum research in Sweden. *International Review of Education,* 11, pp. 189–208.

Härnqvist, K. (1961) The estimation of reserves of ability. In Halsey (ed.) *Ability and Educational Opportunity.* Paris: OECD.

Härnqvist, K. (1966) Social factors and educational choice. *International Journal of the Educational Sciences,* 1, pp. 87–102.

Härnqvist, K. (1968) Relative changes in intelligence from 13 to 18. *Scandinavian Journal of Psychology,* 9, pp. 50–82.

Johannesson, I. (1966) *Tonåringar i skolan: Undersökningarnas allmänna uppläggning, undersökningsinstrument och problemställningar.* (Teenagers in school. General design of the investigations, instruments and problems.) Rep. I. Stockholm: Institute of Education, School of Education.

Johannesson, I. and Magnusson, D. (1960) *Social- och personlighetspsykologiska faktorer i relation till skolans differentiering.* Stockholm: SOU: 42.

Ljung, B. O. and Jansson, S. (1970) Recruitment to the gymnasium in Sweden. *Scandinavian Journal of Educational Research,* 1, pp. 1–14.

Magnusson, D. *et al.* (1966) *Anpassning, beteende och prestation – Örebroprojektet I. Planläggning.* (Adjustment, behaviour and achievement – the Örebro Project I. Design.) Stockholm: Psychology Laboratory of the University of Stockholm.

Malmquist, E. (1958) *Reading Disabilities in the First Grades of the Elementary School.* Stockholm: Almqvist & Wiksell.

Marklund, S. (1962) *Skolklassens storlek och struktur.* (size and structure of the school class.) Stockholm: Almqvist & Wiksell.

Marklund, S. (1968) *Lärarlämplighet: problem och propåer.* (Teacher aptitude: problems and suggestions.) Stockholm: Liber.

Neymark, E. (1961) *Selektiv rörlighet* (Selective migration.) Stockholm: Personaladministrativa rådet.

Norinder, Y. (1946) *Twin Differences in Writing Performance: a study of heredity and school training.* Lund: Håkan Ohlsson.

Norinder, Y. (1957) The evolving comprehensive school in Sweden. *International Review of Education,* 3, pp. 3–20.

Passow, A. (1968) Bureau L4 and educational research and planning in Sweden. Some comments and observations. *School Research,* 9 (1968). Stockholm: Skolöverstyrelsen.

Pedagogisk forskning (Educational research) (1944) Specialnummer i anledning av upprättandet av Psykologisk-pedagogiska institutet. *Skola och samhälle,* 25, pp. 189–230.

Pedagogisk forskning (Educational research) (1955) Specialnummer (5–6). *Skola och samhälle,* 36, pp. 145–85.

Pedagogisk forskning (Educational research) (1968) In *Samhällsforskning: rapporter från fem arbetsgrupper tillsatta av forskningsberedningen.* Lund: Studentlitteratur.

Siegvald, H. (1944) *Experimentella undersökningar rörande intellektuella könsdifferenser.* (Experimental studies in intellectual sex differences.) Lund: Håkan Ohlsson.

Sjöstrand, W. (1961) *Skolberedningen och differentieringsfrågan* Stockholm: Natur & Kultur.

Sjöstrand, W. (1966) *Skolan och demokratin.* (School and democracy.) Malmö: Codex.

Sjöstrand, W. (1967) School achievement and development of personality. In *Paedagogica Europeae*, pp. 189–21.

Skola och samhälle, 31 (1950), pp. 211–17; 36 (1955), pp. 163–8; 41 (1960), pp. 222–30.

Smith, G. (1949) *Psychological Studies in Twin Differences*. Lund: Gleerup.

SNS (1950) *Skolreformen och näringslivet*. (The school reform and the business community.) Stockholm: Studieförbundet Näringsliv och Samhälle.

SOU 1952:33. *Den första lärarhögskolan* (The first school. of education.) Stockholm.

Stukát, K. G. (1966) *Pedagogisk forskningsmetodik*. (Educational research methodology.) Stockholm: Almqvist & Wiksell.

Stukát, K. G. and Engström. R. (1966) *TV-observationer av läraraktiviteter i klassrummet*. Rep. Göteborg: School of Education.

Svensson, N. E. (1962) *Ability Grouping and Scholastic Achievement*. Stockholm: Almqvist & Wiksell

Svensson, N. E. and Björklund, E. (1966) Educational research and development in Sweden. *Educational Sociology*, 39.

Wallin, E. (1968) *Spelling. Factorial and experimental studies*. Stockholm: Almqvist & Wiksell

Wolfle, D. (1954). *America's Resources of Specialized Talent*. New York: Harpers.

Vernon, P. E. (1957) *Secondary School Selection*. London: Methuen.

Index

DATE DUE

NOV 2 5 1975			
DEC 1 5 1975			
AUG 4 1976			
NOV 3 1976			

370
H956L

39459